MORE HEAVEN

BECAUSE EVERY CHILD IS SPECIAL

D1144105

By Jo Anne White PhD

outskirtspress

DENVER, COLORADO

Permission should be addressed in writing to Dr. Jo Anne White at joanne@drjoannewhite.com, 856-795-5854, PO Box 176, Haddonfield, NJ 08033

Outskirts Press, Inc.
http://www.outskirtspress.com

Paperback ISBN: 978-1-4787-6547-9
Hardback ISBN: 978-1-4787-6752-7

Library of Congress Control Number: 2016901893

Outskirts Press and the "OP" logo are trademarks belonging to Outskirts Press, Inc.

PRINTED IN THE UNITED STATES OF AMERICA

Contents

MORE HEAVEN is based on a true-life experiment that began in the Philadelphia school system in the late 1970s in response to the 1975 Education for the Handicapped Act, ruling that public schools in the US educate all children with disabilities, despite their severity. Finally, landmark legislation provided for the civil rights of children with disabilities that had previously been denied.

One such pilot program began in Philadelphia. I was hired by the Board of Education as the sole teacher and program coordinator for children who were expelled or who had never before entered the hallways and classrooms of a public school. Everyone, from the 'regular' education teachers to the principal, seemed nervous and skeptical. Nevertheless, the program began slowly and painstakingly. To everybody's surprise, what began as one classroom burgeoned into two and three in the following years in just that school alone.

The success of our program paved the way for more classes to open in other schools throughout Philadelphia. Not only did we persevere; we conquered skepticism and won victories for these children to live and thrive in society. I fought hard alongside my children and their tireless parents to restore dignity. This dignity, the birthright of every human being, had been unfairly denied them. The time had come to make things right.

Listen to the children's imaginary stories within the main story. At first, they speak of terror, pain, isolation, hopelessness, and loss. As the children become more comfortable with themselves, more familiar with each other, and ready to tackle such acts that we often take for granted, like speaking and relating—something happens. Not only is there an external, noticeable change in their behavior and countenance; there's an internal shift as well. This inner shift is seen in these children's inner fantasies, their imaginations, and play. The internal images and storylines are now less scary, less isolating, and less self-defeating. In the evolving fantasies, there is more acceptance and "normalized" activity such as relating and having fun. As the children venture out with each other, find successes and victories, play together and learn, their imaginary worlds reflect all that back to them while their teacher, Tina, helps them to make sense of it all.

More Heaven was inspired by the children's voices, children who could not always speak for themselves to tell us what they wanted, children who were often so consumed by their own emotions that they could not take one step forward from choice to responsibility.

This book is written for Tracey who walked on her toes, for red-headed, freckled-face Alan who mimicked my words, for Stephan, who cupped his hands over his ears when he heard voices, and for Marcellus, who taught me how to truly laugh at myself.

More Heaven reaches in from the heart outward to all children. They will be heard.

Beginning with Eva

March 8

In my hands are records of a little girl I have never met. Psychological data, medical history, and her family background all tell us Eva's story from birth to seven years. One young life, probed with fine-tuned instruments, and then split open for dissection by impartial fingers.

There is no record of Eva's consent to her life exposed like this. Eva Turner diagnosed as "exhibiting autistic behavior," I wonder what she would tell us. Does she remember that she was delivered from her mother's womb with the aid of forceps? Can she recall when paralysis numbed the right side of her face with three months of no feeling in her right cheek in the first year of her life? What nightmarish visions tormented Eva to leave her crying in her sleep for two stormy years? Does she remember?

"Stay-at-home mom, dad in auto mechanics, and two older brothers, ages 9 and 11," I skim over the pages. "Not able to test for reading, math, or intelligence, lacking social and communication skills and engaging in self-stimulation."

I slip the papers back inside the folder and wonder why, if Eva's language was developing normally, she stopped talking at age 2½.

She will officially start school tomorrow. The moment her feet step on the pavement my responsibility as her teacher begins. A language-delayed little girl with the body of a seven year old and the mental age of a child of three, somehow I am to stir her. I hope she'll be receptive and open to me and willing to listen and learn what I have to teach her. I wonder what marks a child with emotional challenges wears on her face to make her more visible or more hidden than the rest of us. And, I wonder if her secrets are any more secret than my own. Is her fear imprinted across her eyes to remind us of something we want to forget?

March 9

In the back seat of the yellow school bus a head bobs up and down, still moving to the bumps in the road, although the bus is now still. Eva picks up her bag and prances down the bus corridor. She pauses as she reaches the door, eyes wide and blank, then steps out of the bus. The driver smiles for the first time, shaking his head in disbelief.

The bus drives off and we are both left standing there on the curb: stranger to stranger. Swiftly Eva's glazed eyes dart over everything around her: the grass at her feet, the tree next to us under whose leafless branches we are standing. She quickly looks over my leather boots, my skirt, my dark brown hair and the vast school building behind us. She doesn't notice my face or my eyes. I'm not sure what she's really seeing or registering in her mind. The different parts of her body appear loosely held together by nylon threads. Like a marionette without a puppeteer, she hovers in the space in front of me. If I touch her, will the parts of her pull apart?

"Eva," I call to her.

She will not look at me. Her head jerks back and forth, attached to an invisible wire spring.

"Eva, let's go inside."

I am chilly, wrapped only in my blue turtleneck sweater. Eva's red coat is unbuttoned and hanging off her shoulders. She is impervious to the wind and to my voice, more like a wide-eyed spirit who doesn't know what to do in her body, in her humanness. I step towards the door, then turn around to see if Eva is following. Her body is in motion: her arms shaking in front of her, hands cupped, prancing sideways on her toes. She is like a runner rooted to the ground, all movement and energy but going nowhere. "Eva, here, look over here. Let's go into the building."

With reservation I take her hand. Her hand, cool and limp, hangs loosely in my own without acknowledging the touch. I feel like I'm just another object to Eva, one that she's not particularly interested in. All that will change; it has to.

March 11

Eva comes in the same school bus. The bus driver opens the door and leaps out, waiting for Eva to follow, but she doesn't budge.

"C'mon," he whines, "I got somewhere else to go." When he sees me, relief animates his sagging face. "Are you her teacher?"

"Yes, I am," I say.

He is baffled by the notion of educating Eva.

"Believe me," he confides, "I wouldn't want your job for nothin' in this world."

I believe him and watch when he uncomfortably shifts his weight onto his left foot and stuffs his calloused hands into his jacket pocket. Eva hops down the bus steps and smells the railing. The bus driver looks at me with a mixture of pity and disbelief. Wearily he shakes his head, reinforcing his words, as he climbs back onto the bus and closes the door.

Eva and I walk inside the building past the main office. Black curls swing rhythmically with the repetitive turns of Eva's head. She hums a low atonal chant.

"Eva, this is our classroom," I tell her as I unlock the door to the room.

She rushes past me dancing on her toes, a tightrope walk in space. Around the room Eva runs, touching and sniffing the walls in each of the four corners. She giggles; her fingers twitch in nervous staccato brushes of the air. Dancing, talking fingers. Who is listening, and who is talking? Is there a melody playing inside her I cannot hear, a voice inside her instructing, like the caller of the square dance?

"Eva, we will come here every day and do nice things together. We will paint, read stories, play with clay."

The soft humming is now louder, insistent, muffling my words with angry chanting: a clever design to tune me out and distance from me. Barriers of sound cushion Eva from an external world so that no other sounds may filter through the walls.

I raise my voice to compete with the humming, yet am careful not to alter my tone. I will make myself heard but I will not impose my will.

"Eva, each day when you come to school we will look at pictures, we will eat together."

Eva's fists pummel her head; the anger turns inward. If she beats herself, if she bruises her fingers and her head, then maybe I'll stop. Maybe I will go away. I am an intruder, ripping through her surrounding walls and into Eva's space with my words. I must remain outside the fiberglass fortress she's constructed. The entranceways are sealed; there is no way in and no way out of the labyrinth of her soul.

When I am silent, Eva's self-inflicted blows cease. She runs around the room weaving circles, faster and faster. As if from a merry-go-round, the classroom must now appear a strange and precarious world of blurring light and color, with shapes and patterns, myself included—blending together, form into form, as she whizzes by. Maybe this is merely a sped-up version of Eva's regular ride, a light and sound show that never slows down long enough for the lone rider to get off. How does she differentiate the objects from one another? How can she feel herself on the ground with everything whizzing by? It's dizzying just to watch her.

Eventually she will tire herself, I wish patiently, waiting for her taut and energized body to slacken with weariness. Eva's face is lit with pleasure, a dancer's moment of exaltation, a shaman's ecstasy. Unmarred by conventions, she enters a room for the first time and fills up the space with her moving self. A world she creates in and of herself. Is this enough? No one else is needed for the completion of the dance. Eva is the one lone rider circuiting around the silent merry-go-round.

Eva stops dancing. She sits on the floor inside the cocoon of circles like any other child engrossed in play but Eva is not playing. Her body rocks forward and backward; her humming is as subdued as a lullaby. The black patent leather shoes, creased and slightly scuffed, lay at the doorway to the room where she kicked them off in the midst of her frenzied activity.

I will venture slowly and wait for a signal to enter. Surely there are windows in the fortress I can peer into, cracks that Eva peeks out from. I hope that I'll know how to find these peepholes to read the messages chiseled on the walls inside.

I do not trespass and the morning is couched in our separateness. The lunches arrive with a young boy who curiously eyes Eva now gazing vacantly into her hands.

"I brought your lunches," he says, handing me the warm aluminum dishes.

"Thank you." I'm glad for any exchange of words. I place the lunches on the back table and call to Eva.

"Here are our lunches. Are you hungry, Eva? Let's get ready to eat now."

No answer. I wash my hands at the sink, sit down and unwrap my lunch. If she's hungry maybe she will come to the table. The choice is hers. I nibble on the pasty macaroni and Eva stops examining her hand. Now her attention and senses are heightened as she sizes up the changes to our situation and my shift away from her to my own activity. Closer to the table she inches; her nostrils flare in anticipatory alarm. I take the foil cover off Eva's lunch and place her meal opposite mine. Eva stares at the food, then darts away again to the other side of the room. Her black curls swing with the quick turns of her head.

I feign total absorption in my lunch; I will not stare at her. I will not see her as she licks the blackboard with her tongue.

Again, Eva runs laterally across the room and back to the table.

Still standing, she grabs a handful of macaroni and shovels it into her mouth. The macaroni is forced down in gulps. Eva reaches for another handful before the bulges in her cheeks disappear. Fingers, drenched in tomato sauce, press the peas and carrots into her swelling mouth. Some of the vegetables fall to the floor and Eva scoops them up in her hand. She slaps them mashed and soiled against her lips and sucks in the food noisily. Eva grabs for my roll.

"Eva, this is my lunch. You have yours. You may not take my roll without asking me first." I gently disentangle the roll from her clenched fingers. Her wrists and her head shake angrily; she tugs at the long dark braids of her own hair. This is the dance of anger. I consume the remains of my own lunch and wipe up the peas and carrots, tomato sauce and spit from the table and the floor.

Someday, someday soon, Eva will sit at a table and eat lunch with me.

March 14

I have not recorded anything about Eva for days. Not because I've overlooked the six hours each day we spend together. These hours overflow into the other waking hours of my life. This little girl is vivid in my thoughts, my internal imagery. I see her face in my night-dreams and in my dream-stricken waking moments. Her eyes, so large with fear, are an apparition I cannot shake from my consciousness.

Nothing is different; nothing is changed since my last journal entry. Eva comes to school in the same yellow bus, driven by the same bus driver and the ritual of the dance is repeated each day. The dance is not staged for me. I am the onlooker; my hands are empty of applause.

Today is the first day I notice the echolalia, the parrot-like mimicry of my words. Eva's voice is ashen and cold, recently roused from its burial place. There is no emotion; her small voice is flattened by years of interment.

"Hello, Eva," I say to her in greeting.

"Hello, Eva," she echoes.

"How are you today?"

"—are you today?"

My words are arrows which fall short of my target. I'm aware of their impotence when they are dully repeated to me; symbols of sound she does not decipher. I must decode the symbols of her world before I can offer her my own.

My parents just called tonight, eager to find out all about my new job but I didn't say much except that Eva is different than any child I've ever encountered in my previous three years of teaching. Dad, already a tenured science teacher, offered his advice that it will take time. "Take copious notes," he suggested, reminding me of the scientific method of inquiry that he judiciously follows. Well, Eva's not a lab rat, not that dad would ever think like that, but he did have a point. Keeping notes, tracking Eva's behavior and running academic assessments when and if Eva's ready will give me more information than I have right now. That I can do; I already have practice. But what can I do about her strange behavior, her animal-like sounds? What about the stimming and flapping movements and how she doesn't respond to any direction — at least not from me?

Peeking Inside the Fortress

March 20

Of Eva's world I have glimpses. I spend one half hour whirling in my living room; I dance as I have seen Eva dance. Her speed and her energy I cannot match. I'm so dizzy and uncomfortably near the edge of losing control. In whirling, there is only the energetic motion. The couch and the plants, the chairs and the ceiling collide with one another and blur. There is nothing to root them into constancy or separation. My perception of space is altered. Everything is fleeting and fluid; my body spins and my thoughts cascade off me like falling leaves. As I lose my grip on the external world, as it melts and swims around me, I feel the essence of myself in flight. It is joyful and it is light. Thank you, Eva. And yet, I also understand how disembodied she must feel when in motion. Her body parts moving, but seemingly unconnected and disjointed when she whirls. How does she even have a sense of herself, her wholeness amidst all this fragmentation? Is that how the world appears to her, how I appear? With more questions than answers, I'm resigned to do more research in the classroom and outside to find out as much as I can about Eva and autism.

Today Eva is more distressed than I've seen her. She doesn't dance but sits rocking on the bare floor. With her eyes pinched shut and her personal soundscape switched on, she anesthetizes any sensation of discomfort. The song Eva hums is plaintive, issuing from within the deep cavernous wealth inside of her. I want to soothe her but I cannot go past the walls. Visible kernels of pain spread across Eva's face in silent tears. Eva awakens from her reverie just minutes before the bus comes to transport her home.

March 21

Eva's smiling face reveals nothing of yesterday's requiem. She hums and prances to the classroom. I am near her but I can feel that the distance between us is vast. Once inside the room, Eva runs from me. The room is familiar to Eva. I am as familiar, but no more so than other recognizable objects—the desks and the chairs. Right now there's no palpable link to bind us together.

"Daily News, Daily News," Eva chants inside her cupped hand.

I almost see the newsboy on the corner, newspapers in his hands. I hear him as he calls to the passersby. Where is Eva's voice; in which part of the fortress is it hidden?

I am learning the recordings in Eva's head. Words and conversations, the memory tapes she reels off. They distract her and provide oral pleasure. A medley of sounds shields Eva from a world she disclaims.

Eva can reproduce conversations of others she's siphoned through the walls. She sings them; she chants and whispers them to the blackboard and to her fingers. They roll inside her mouth and, as her tongue trips over them, Eva laughs.

When I question Eva, only my question is repeated.

With the clay on the table, can I entice her?

"Look, Eva. Look at the clay. It feels so smooth. See, I roll it and bend it and pull it apart."

Eva inserts her fingers into her mouth and then smells them. First I roll the clay into a ball, a snake. I mold it into a cat. Her eyes dart to the clay and then recede inside where the voices call her back. She listens. She obeys them. When they whisper to her she giggles nervously; I believe she is frightened of them. As the outsider, I'm more terrifying than the voices.

> *They tell her they are friends and will never leave her. They denounce the teacher as her betrayer who will coil the hissing body of the clay snake*

around her neck till she is not breathing.

'Don't listen, don't listen,' the voices murmur against her hair.

Their breath blows cool and then hot. She is sweltering and begs them to stop as the fire scorches her. She dances to wrest herself free from the glow-ing flames. She puts out their breath with the salt of her sweat.

They swallow the granules of salt till their mouths parch and their nostrils cake with white crystals. From deep within her liquefying body, she hums to them as they slumber.

"Look at the cat, Eva. Look at his tail. Isn't his tail long?" My voice explodes in her head.

"Isn't his tail long; isn't his tail long; isn't his tail long."

"—Tail long," Eva mimics me.

"Touch it, Eva. Don't you want to touch the clay?"

The cat of clay will claw your face, they threat-en. The cat's sandpaper tongue will score your body, scraping layers of skin off the bones. She believes them.

I stretch clay into silent animals. The lion's mouth implodes in a hushed roar. The sea lion waits poised for the slippery fish never thrown. They remain motionless on the table where I have left them. Their melody is voiceless; the silent music pacifies her.

On the floor, ten feet from Eva, I sit and rock my body in time with hers. Once again I'm in motion, exploring my own physical experience as I imitate Eva. Soothed by the undulations of my body, thoughts detach from meaning and sensation runs through me like blood. If I close my eyes, I imagine myself a child. I smell, hear, feel, and taste everything. There are no words. Sounds have colors. Some smells tickle my nose; others I taste in my mouth. I perceive from the inside out. The world is an umbilical cord woven to my center. Is this what everything feels like to Eva? Or, maybe the movement makes it easier for her to handle all the sensory bombardment. I don't really know. When my eyes open, Eva is watching me. She quickly averts her eyes, raises herself off the floor and hides in the coat closet. Eva pushes the door shut. Her thin wax-like legs and white stocking feet are visible beneath the double doors.

"Bogey man, Bogey man," I hear her whisper to the darkness.

March 26

She haunts me; she taunts me. I am spellbound by her loveliness, her soul of silken music. Yet, I am terrified of her capacity for self-affliction and her voices. I have no antidote either for her fear or for my own. I am a teacher on the edge of a deep precipice. Inviting in revelations of Eva's world, while I try to pry open the parts of her that are inhabited by nameless, faceless, invisible creatures of darkness.

> *The walls of the fortress are clammy when she bumps into them: ice water from the cellar will drown her if she sleeps too long. In the fortress she is not alone, they are always with her.*
>
> *She wakes to the voices sloshing around in her ear—a reminder like the sun staining her eyes with orange spots, that it is morning.*
>
> *In the evening, while she sleeps, the voices hook inside the bones of her head and pound her skull with a steel hammer.*

I hope I'll have the courage to reach out my hand in a moment of Eva's frenzy and be strong enough to battle for both of us. Will I be able to gaze upon the sludge of her nightmares without running from them? I have not forgotten the beauty of Eva's world, the motion, the poetry of her limbs. Do I have a right to defend her specialness despite accusation of collusion? Once I'm inside the fortress, will I lose resolve and forget why I am there? Perhaps I'll be tempted and want to linger too long. Will I bed down with dreams I shall never awaken from? I hope I'll have the strength to take Eva by the hand and lead us both out into the sunlight.

March 28

I rock on the floor when Eva rocks on the floor; I dance when she dances. My imitation does not deter her whirlwind form. I have converted the silence into a musical recital. I set the stage, provide the props for the dances. I am among the cast. In order of appearance there is Eva and myself.

Whirling, whirling has its own sense of time, its own measure. I copy Eva's body, replicating her movements with my own. This is how I greet her. I fight to draw her out; she is adrift somewhere my spoken voice cannot find her. My hand stumbles along in the darkness; my fingers tickle her stomach lightly and Eva giggles. She runs from me. The closet is her refuge when my presence jolts her. I am always lurking outside the fortress. Never sleeping, guardian of the walls, I watch and prowl about the exteriors.

I roll a small rubber bouncing ball under the raised door into the closet. It smacks against the edges and rebounds. Eva scratches the walls with her fingernails. A grating sound, anger so controlled that I shudder. The ball disappears and reappears. Eva will not touch it. Over and over the ball bounces between us, a game of fingers and hands. Silently the game is played. The opponents are invisible to each other. Only Eva's stick legs, white ankle socks topped with a frill of lace, and scuffed black patent leather shoes are visible from the other side of the closet door. The game is powered by Eva's decision not to roll the ball to me. The scratching stops. I roll the ball and wait for its return. No ball. Eva's grabbed it. Seconds later the ball, still wet from Eva's mouth, rolls to me. I propel the pink ball toward the interiors of the darkness; Eva pushes it through the slim opening, back from the other side.

Okay, so it's not much for a seven year old to do, according to some benchmarks, but what happened today is exhilarating. This is the first time there's been any interaction between Eva and me. Who cares if the closet served as a divider between us? Something big is taking place here—real play, non-verbal communication, one-on-one contact and I marvel at all of it while reminding myself this is a beginning.

March 30

Today I dance closer to Eva. I want my nearness to become more real than whatever separates us. Eva knows I'm there. Her movements are more frenetic but she doesn't move away from me.

Magically the watery streaks I paint on the blackboard appear and disappear. Two cups of water are set on the paint tray.

"Look, Eva, I'm making a little girl. Look at my picture. Next, I'll make a tree and a bird." I speak to disperse the gloom of our silence.

"See my fingers, Eva, they are painting."

My drawings completed, I move away but the cups remain. Enough time passes, Eva bends over a cup, smells and dunks her finger inside. She tastes the water then picks up the cup. Her tongue encircles the cup's edges. Eva pours water onto the floor and slaps at the moving puddle she's created. I fill the sink with warm water and soap suds. Cups and boats and plastic bottles float on top of the rising bubbles.

"Water, water, bubbles of water," I sing and splash.

In the center of the floor Eva stands shaking her hands, her eyes glued to her moving fingers.

"Come on, Eva, don't you want to play in the water? It feels so warm and bubbly."

I squirt water into the basin, holding the plastic bottle high, exaggerating my movements like an actor on the stage playing to an audience who is not watching. I know she hears me.

Sidestepping on her toes, Eva is behind me, her eyes riveted to the basin. The boat coasts through the water.

> *'Don't touch it. Don't touch it,' voices whisper inside her moving fingers.*
> *'The water will eat through your body like acid. Fingers and hands will dissolve and your body will melt until nothing is left but your disappearing face,' they warn her. 'Don't listen to her or you'll be sorry,' they threaten.*

Eva sniffs the water, looking fleetingly at my fingers skating through the suds.

"Touch the water. Don't you want to touch the water, Eva?"

"Water, Eva," she repeats my words.

Eva forcibly twists her body away from the sink and the conflicting noises in her head. Voices, there are always the voices. Now another voice enters the fortress beyond her ears and behind her eyes; the voice of the teacher serenely inviting, a voice that promises not to vanish or retreat.

Eva smashes her hands against the table, overturns chairs and rushes to the menagerie of clay left standing. She seizes the lion and the cat and slams them to the floor. She pulls the sea lion up to her mouth and bites off his head, sputtering clay pieces onto her yellow flowered dress. Clay bits fly everywhere. Eva hurls them at the blackboard and the closet. She picks up a piece of the clay and grazes her cheek against it, then flattens the clay with her fingers. Eva stares at the clay by raising her hands close up to her squinting eyes. The clay is not hot. The clay has not burned her. Soft and cool against her face and her fingers; have the voices lied to her?

Eva slips to the floor, covers her ears with her hands and whimpers like a wounded animal.

I walk cautiously to where Eva lies in a heap and crouch down two feet from her and hum. Eva's head is still lowered but the spasms in her body subside. Instinctively my hand reaches out to comfort. Eva's body stiffens like the arched and bristly back of a cat. Her warning signal: Don't get any closer. Don't come too near. Don't touch.

I retract my hand and self-consciously smooth down my hair, still humming the lullaby:

"Tender shepherd, tender shepherd
Won't you let me count your sheep?
One in the meadow, two in the garden
Three in the nursery fast asleep."

One Month On

April 4

I can't believe April's here already. I have worked with Eva almost one full month, five days a week, six hours a day with one little girl. I have three children on my roster. The school cannot locate Patty, the other little girl. Every day I'm told that Ricardo is coming tomorrow; every tomorrow Ricardo never shows.

I see Eva more than I see anyone else. Thirty-five hours a week in the presence of one other person. No one relieves me; no one fills in for me.

"But you only have one child," they insist.

"Yes I know I only have one child but do you know what being with that one child all day without a break is like?"

"We'll get back to you." The phone clicks.

I feel as if I'm a visitor to a remote and sparsely inhabited island and I have found a native dancing in the woods. Her language and customs are new to me, stranger than any I have ever known. She is like a sylph bewitched, she runs wildly through the silhouetted trees. I trail her phosphorescent glimmer. She leaves no traces behind. In and out of a sylvan wood she darts, talking to her gods with trembling fingers. I am the freak, one of the shadow people. I am the phantom walking in darkness. She photographs me through the hidden cameras inside her eyes. Always sensing me, knowing my movements; does she know my thoughts as well?

One child. We eat together; we go to the bathroom together. I've been advised never to leave Eva alone. Has she been instructed to do the same? No other reality but Eva's and mine. If I tell my colleagues that sometimes when I talk with friends the echolalia steals into my voice, will they think I've gone mad? If I reveal that I've experimented with Eva's world, what label would they scribble across my face?

Eva's not as fragile as she looks. Sometimes I think it's a pose. When I look again, Eva's outstretched on the floor, blankly staring out of a glazed smile like some crazed enchanted princess. Rapture or insensibility; I can't be sure. What magical incantations do I recite to break the spell? "Here lies Eva. Heal her. Here lies Eva with arms flapping, offer her a song."

Mr. Bell, the janitor, carries in a rug on his shoulders. Eva doesn't look up until he leaves; then she circles around the new nesting place like a bat. Eva flops onto the rug and giggles into the weave. Her ear is pressed against the fuzzy bronze carpet listening to the fast continuous stream of blood which is pumped inside her head by an unknown source. I narrow the physical distance between us and Eva draws herself up, wary of my approaching footsteps.

"Do you like the new rug, Eva? Now you can sit on the rug rather than the cold floor."

"Rug Eva, rug Eva, rug Eva," her mechanical voice churns in my ears. Do the words even make sense to her? Does she understand their meaning or is the repetition just something that she has to do and has no real control over? Does it relieve emotional or physical tension? How will I ever be sure?

April 6

Eva gestures in the direction of the door when she wants to go to the bathroom. We go silently together; Eva runs ahead. With the bathroom door slightly ajar, I wait outside. The humming begins and I hear the water dripping from the faucet Eva has turned on. The toilet flushes repeatedly—one, two, three times. I let Eva flush it; I allow her to perform her rituals to feel safe and not judged by me. I give her time to be Eva and accept her as she is. Of course, there are behaviors to change and work that will challenge her, and I hope that she's capable. Sometimes I sense so much more intelligence behind the frenetic movement, the animal sounds and the ritualistic behaviors that she displays. And at other times, I have my doubts and wonder how I'll ever get through to her. I know that I've signed up for the task and don't regret it, only sometimes I wonder at the magnitude of it all.

"Come on, Eva. Let's finish up in the bathroom. It will be time to eat lunch soon."

I peek in to see what Eva is up to. Her head is down between her legs and she's looking into the bowl.

"Are you ready now, Eva?"

Giggling and squirming, Eva looks up at me for a split second and then her eyes are cast downward again as though it never happened. The eye contact, I mean. It was amazing, although it lasted only seconds, she looked right into my eyes because she wanted to and she initiated it. Yes to small victories. Yes! And then the questions fire up because how can I really be sure. In my eagerness to relate and make contact with Eva, did I see only what I wanted to see? Did I make it up? "Get a grip, Tina, you can't lose it now," I say.

I wonder if there's a hallowed quality to a place that's connected up with our bodies, where restrictions and taboos are suspended and private selves exposed.

April 8

Eva is not in school today. Not knowing what's happened to Eva is disconcerting and the break in our routine makes me feel uncomfortable. When I dial her number, an operator tells me it's disconnected. Disconnected and beleaguered by the crossfire in my own mind, I feel uncertain of what I do here. Where is Eva? Perhaps they've called a meeting and decided that I was an unfit teacher and have withdrawn Eva from school. Maybe Eva's mother has determined this is all the time required to "heal" her little girl and I will never see Eva again.

Annoying and disconcerting doubts surface temporarily about my abilities as a teacher. They appear seemingly to dislodge my confidence as a teacher, but they won't succeed. Have I missed the mark with Eva? Something is absent from our flow together and I have to figure out what that is. The gnawing questions serve me because they become the basis for inquiry which I know is so much a part of learning and testing information. Dad, bless his scientific mind and recent reminder, would be proud of me. See Dad, I listened to you, after all. And, as always I'm glad I did.

When was the last time I called home and spoke to my parents? It seems like ages ago, so much has happened and yet so little. I've been so wrapped up in trying to break through Eva's impenetrable walls that my social life has taken a nosedive and my familial obligations as well. I know Mom and Dad want to know how I'm doing with teaching and if there's anything new, like a new love interest on the horizon. Love — as if I have the emotional strength for it after battling with Eva's demons and feeling as isolated as she must feel. I'll talk to them tonight. They'll make me feel better and connected again to life, to people and real conversation.

I realize I don't want to be a sugar technician and hold out my hand with a strand of M&M's to tie around Eva's heart. If I offer a piece of candy to Eva, greedily she ingests it, dully performing the required task. Mechanically everything is fine but gone is the spontaneity and the magic. I want our interaction to be real and I want to explore the cellular makeup of her fortress as she shows me the way. I don't want to be placated by the rote acceptance of sweets, nor do I want to be fooled by Eva's submissiveness because she wants a tangible reward. Yes, behavior management works and is a valuable tool that I've used effectively. But, there's more to learning and interacting than just that and I aim to make that happen. Having a tenacious nature is a plus, plugging and plugging away without giving up easily—that's me. It has to pay off, it just has to.

April 12

When I first see Eva today, I have to stifle a cry of surprise. Her hair is uncombed and hangs in stiff knots about her head. Her pink cotton blouse is wrinkled and soiled and her cracked black patent leather shoes are on the wrong feet. As she hops down from the bus I immediately sense a difference. Her body seems somehow smaller and her walk and movements more cautious, quieter. She barely lifts her feet as she steps and doesn't seem to recognize me as I lead her up the stairs.

"Hi, Eva," the secretaries call to her; they're baffled by her daily repetitive response.

"Hi, Eva," she echoes almost inaudibly, looking past everyone.

I have to strain to hear her voice. The book bag falls down on the stairs, but Eva doesn't notice it's slipped out of her hands.

"Eva, you dropped your book bag. Don't you want it?" Eva's head shakes from side to side. Does she hear my words?

> *Inside the fortress there are no demarcations. Shapeless voices float attached to heads without bodies. There are no eyes. Mouths open and close and thick darkness swallows up the words. Pellets of sound wound her as they thrash against the soft walls of her head. Too loud and the walls will come down.*

I wave my hand in front of Eva's face; her eyes do not blink. They stare emptily outward through a translucent film; wires fasten them inside.

I bend down to retrieve the book bag and we walk inside the room in a haunted silence. Eva's body twitches in front of me and she whirls around the rug as around a funeral pyre, igniting the fire with the heat of her fingers.

On the rug Eva lies, her body flat against the wooly mass like paint splayed onto a canvas. She hears her breath thump in her head and feels it pulsate through her arms. Something inside her is alive and moving; something pounds against the walls. She is terrified but it never ceases. Louder and softer, quick and then slow as though whatever is inside her is dying.

"Boogey man, bogey man, no John, now you done it, Star Wars," the tapes spill from Eva's mouth. Eva pounds the floor with her fists. I hear her sobbing.

"No, John, no John!" I scream into the floor like Eva.

She tunes me out, self-absorbed in a world I'm not privy to yet. I feel as though she watches me to sense my whereabouts and to sense safety or danger. Eva cocks her head and briefly follows my movements with her eyes. In and out I fade like an unfocused shadow across her retina.

April 15

When Eva is inside the room, she seizes the edge of the carpet and tries to wrap herself inside it. Under the carpet Eva slides with only her head visible.

"Eva, Eva, Eva," I sing. I reach under the carpet and tickle Eva who squirms but doesn't pull away from me. Eva's body wriggles closer.

"I'm going to tickle you," I tell her. My fingers zoom playfully and gently into her back.

"I'm going to tickle your stomach. Where's your stomach, Eva? Come on, where's your stomach hiding?"

I exaggerate my words; my voice rises and falls with deliberate inflection. Eva squeals; she shimmies further down inside the space where rug and floor meet. Further away from me Eva advances, but now for the purpose of play.

"Where's Eva? Where's Eva?" I chant. "Here I come."

Before my fingers make contact with her body, Eva laughs. With the carpet raised, I poke my head under.

"Oh, Eva, where are you?" I call.

Inside, where Eva is quiet and huddled, I venture. Eva's head is bent, her body twitches excitedly.

"Oh, Eva, Eva." Eva looks at me. Our eyes touch. The moment comes and then is gone.

Sometimes, I feel so alone in this relationship of student and teacher. Yet, I can't deny the progress that's happening. Eva trusts me a little more than before, becoming curious about me and my zany sense of playfulness. I will engage her and continue to earn her trust. She'll become more comfortable with my world as I learn more of hers.

April 18

Physically, the distance between us narrows. No eye contact, but I can reach out my arm and touch her. Eva licks everything.

"Stick out your tongue, Eva, let me see your tongue. Where is it, Eva? Where's your tongue hiding?" I playfully chant with my fingers close to her lips.

Eva doesn't resist an object so near to her mouth without tasting it. Her tongue darts out like a probe. When I move my hand away she searches for the vanishing fingers and has to find them with her eyes. Eva giggles, leaving bubbles of saliva on my fingers as an offering. I don't draw back my hand. I don't flinch from her wetness. Eva leans her body into me and then quickly runs to the chalkboard smearing saliva across the charcoal surface with her long fingers.

"Now you've done it. Now you've done it."

> *There's a room inside the fortress; a room she*
> *may not enter, where they live and breed. The voices*
> *multiply and fester in one room she's never seen.*
> *If she is bad, if she listens to the teacher, they will*
> *show her.*

"What have you done, Eva? What is it? Tell me what you have done."

"—done Eva?"

April 24

In the hallway, Eva runs from me into the first open classroom: the school library. There's already a class in there. Children are scattered searching for books or sitting on chairs or cushions, reading quietly to each other, or silently to themselves. Rushing sideways to the shelf, Eva peels magazines and newspapers off the top. They fly to the floor and some she sweeps up in her arms while prancing side to side. The other children in the library laugh and watch Eva. Fear is in some of their eyes, others look puzzled.

Eva doesn't notice the other occupants of the room. She wants the papers, and glides out as unexpectedly as when she entered.

"I'm terribly sorry," I apologize to the librarian.

"Uh, that's okay," she hesitates uncomfortably. "Is there anything the matter?"

"No. Everything's fine, just fine. Thank you."

The library door shuts loudly behind me. I dash off down the corridor in search of Eva who is not about to give up the papers.

"Eva, these papers are not yours. We have to give them back."

"—them back."

"Yes, we have to give them back and put them where you found them." Eva's hand clenches around the papers and she bites her bottom lip, rubbing the toe of one scuffed shoe around the white-cottoned ankle of her other leg.

"Eva, we have to return the papers."

She grinds her teeth and flees.

"Come on, Eva. Give them to me. The papers are not Eva's. They're not Miss Tina's."

Eva turns away. The humming starts up again. I am no longer

there; Eva doesn't hear me anymore. I will not go away even though she has dismissed me.

"Eva, if you won't give them to me I'll have to take them from you. I'd rather you give them to me."

Eva steps back and I grab the papers from her. Eva pulls fiercely. When I see the anger flash in her eyes, I wince. Because I am stronger, I have the papers.

"Bad Eva, bad Eva." The right tape is released and the recording whirrs around above my head. "Bad Eva, bad Eva."

"No, Eva, you're not bad." I reason with the recording. "Eva's not bad."

I reach out and stroke Eva's head. She lets me.

April 29

I wake up this morning from a violent dream that I'm unable to shake off all day. In the dream, I'm sitting on a train watching other people mutely read the newspapers and stare into gray-filled spaces. When the train stops, a little girl, with long black hair, steps out into the aisle. Her back is to me. I watch her animated body dance unconstrained. A revolver shot pierces the silence. People scream and rush into each other. Someone is knocked down; someone falls down. A young boy shrieks, "My sister, my sister, they've shot my sister." He leans into the legs of the crowd. There on the cold floor of the train the little girl lies as if asleep. Her mouth is plastered in a fixed smile. The boy leans over her face and sobs into her raven-black hair. Without the hair in front of her eyes, I see who is murdered. The boy lifts Eva up and the people move aside to make room for them. His shirt has dark red blotches over the front of it. I look down at my hands, they are covered with blood.

I am amazed that Eva has become so much more than a part of my waking life. Somehow she's touched a place deeper inside. Eva's infiltrated my inner world and has entered my dreams. When I think about it, it's really not surprising. I probably see her more than anyone else now, and the intensity of trying to make real contact with her is great. My job extends so much beyond academics, which are important and aren't ignored. To reach her, gain her trust, and find a way to communicate and to understand her world, have also become primary elements of the instruction.

May 2

Eva speaks to me without words, her breathing and her laughter call to me. When I sleep I hear her screams and I am powerless to stop them. She is steeping slowly into my every moment and further into my dreams. I am again troubled by memories of a night-dream, haunted by its visions. In the dream, I tell my friends I am going away and may not return. I invite them to watch me deepen the abyss I sink into. Surrounded by a thick, dark cobalt blue enveloping cloud, I fall backwards into the darkness. Eva greets me from the other side. She runs laughingly away for me to catch her. She is too quick, I fall again and spin. Everything is bottomless. Above me the stars quake uncomfortably. Eva, Eva, I plead. Where are you? Her invisible laughter consoles me.

The dream follows me around in my waking hours while I try to shake the visions and echoes from my mind. I wonder if the dream has anything to do with feeling frustrated with the progress we're making as we take one step forward and two or three back.

In school today Eva is quiet, absorbing everything without words. She runs to the classroom door which I take as a signal to go the bathroom. She has trouble with the doorknob. I turn it and the door opens. Eva prances outside, just ahead of me in the right direction. I go inside the bathroom with Eva, sit on the floor and sing to her. Eva looks at me and then self-consciously gazes away again. She switches off the overhead light. In the darkness I call to her.

"Who turned off the light, Eva? It's dark in here."

No answer. I call out again to her.

"Oh, Eva, Eva!"

My eyes adjust to the outline of her. The only sound is her teeth as they grate against themselves. The rhythm of her breath is irregular; first comes the rapid panting. Then Eva holds in the air, afraid to let go of it, and the air mounts in her lungs. She fights against expelling parts of herself. If all of her is flushed out with the breath, she will be dispossessed.

> *They tell her they need more room in the fortress. They are overrun with themselves. There is only one more piece of her they want. Give in, they prod her. Give in and it will be over.*

Eva wipes herself and smells her fingers.

"Stinks," she says quietly.

"Yes, Eva. It does stink," I manage to say calmly realizing that Eva is speaking to me as never before.

"It's okay that it smells, Eva, mine does too. Everyone's does."

She regards me closely to discern how I respond to her words, her excrement and her poking of her genitals. Could I love and accept the dirtiest, darkest, most mysterious part of her?

She speaks to me; she speaks to me in the darkness, only one word is uttered. Yet, in that one word alone we have crossed another boundary.

May 7

Eva climbs into my lap and smells my hair. She looks at me then scrambles away.

"See here, Eva. Look at the car." I point to the picture in the magazine.

"Car, Eva."

I turn the page.

"And look, here's a man and a woman. Look, they're eating ice cream." I smack my lips in imitation.

Eva laughs at my noisemaking and moves closer to examine and sniff the colorful page.

"Did you ever see such a tall building, Eva? See how high the building is!"

"—building Eva."

"Yes, it has so-oo-oo many windows."

Eva wanders back inside. I hear myself echo the same words, the same thoughts, insistently, one right after another with no reprieve.

Eva whispers into her hand. "No Eva, no Eva," she shrieks out loud.

> *She hears the walls crack and crumble as they*
> *push through to divest her of herself.*
> *   'Bad Eva, bad Eva,' they chide her. They will*
> *punish her for listening to the other, the outsider's*
> *voice, the voice of the teacher.*

Eva claws her face and cries. She tears the magazine from my hands and flings it across the room.

"Bad Eva, bad Eva."

"Not bad, Eva's not bad," I plead. "Don't be afraid, Eva. You're not bad." Eva slams into my chest with her fists.

"Not bad Eva. You're not bad." I gently but firmly hold onto her wrists to prevent further assault. Eva tries to bite me.

"No, you don't have to hurt me. You don't need to hurt yourself. Eva's not bad."

I hold her in my arms till the weeping subsides. Eva runs into the closet and spends the rest of the morning shut into the unlit enclosure whispering inside her fingers.

May 8

Today there is less humming than yesterday, less tuning out. There doesn't seem to be any evenness to Eva. There are moments when she's right here with me and then other times when I lose her. To what, I'm never sure.

Visiting the Darkness,
Accessing the Light

May 9

"Bogey man, bogey man," Eva whispers inside her cupped hand. Who is the mythical man who fills her with terror? Does he lurk everywhere in Eva's world, in every stranger's face? When Eva is asleep does he come to her, the incubus of her nightmares?

"Bogey man," Eva repeats to her moving fingers.

"Who is the bogey man, Eva?"

I walk to the closet where the art supplies are kept, slide the clay out of its plastic wrapping, and sit down at the table.

"Bogey man," I repeat as though it were some magical charm to infuse the clay with bogey-man attributes.

My fingers tease the soft clay and a face rapidly begins to take shape. A mouth leers into a hideous scowl. Eyes bulge out of the grey skull and a nose protrudes.

"Bogey man." With my fists I pound the clay and chant, "There is no bogey man; there is no bogey man. There is no bogey man."

The bogey man is now a flattened sad-grey piece of clay. Eva inches nearer to look at the bashed-in creature on the table. She takes my hand and guides it to the clay.

"What is it, Eva? What do you want? What do you want me to do?"

Eva's body tenses, the dance stirs in her feet.

"Tell me what is it you want?"

She won't let go of my hand, but squeezes and pushes it into the clay.

"What do you want me to do with the bogey man, Eva?"

"—Bogey man, Eva."

"You want me to make the bogey man?"

I start to press and pull the clay into another loathsome shape.

"Now what, Eva? What do you want me to do?"

"Make bogey man."

She squirms and shakes her hands in front of her face. This is something she wants, something she needs me to do for her.

"Tell me, Eva. Tell me what you want."

"Make eyes."

I make his eyes. Outwardly I am calm, only containing my excitement as Eva speaks to me.

"What next, Eva? What do you want me to do now?"

"Make ears."

His ears I make long and his mouth thick. I endow him with arms and hands and legs—everything that Eva suggests and more. I want the bogeyman to be as real as he is imaginary and dispel as much fear from her as I can.

"Now what should I do with the bogey man, Eva?"

"Kill bogey man."

"Help me, Eva."

I take her hand in mine and mash his eyes deep into his head. Our intertwined hands pummel him out of existence.

"There is no bogey man," I chant. "There is no bogey man. We killed him. Eva and Miss Tina killed the bogey man!"

"No bogey man."

Eva laughs into my eyes.

May 10

Eva hears me recite from the open storybook. We've established a morning routine. Usually for the morning stories, Eva's attentive but not today.

"No story. No story!" she screams to my surprise.

I'm sitting on our carpet and continue to read aloud despite the outburst. She's not testing me, this time; Eva's distraught. The challenge is that she doesn't confide in me. Without her telling me outright, it's not easy to know what's bothering Eva. I have to find out what's wrong; it would be easier to help her if I only knew. Is she sick or troubled; is something not right at home? Maybe it's time to contact her mother again and learn what's up.

Eva rips up papers and scatters them over the floor. Crayons snap. She flings the wax pieces to the floor. Debris crashes around me as she wipes her arms across the tops of several tables, sending markers, Lego pieces, magazines, building blocks, and clay flying in all directions.

"Okay, Eva, now you'll have to pick them up. I know you didn't want to hear the story and you're angry with me. But now you'll have to pick all the toys up. We can't leave toys on the floor like that."

"Eva did that. Eva did that." Her voice is shrill and speeded up. She runs around the room, shaking her fingers hard and fast in front of her. She's not listening to me.

"We'll have to get these toys up, Eva. You'll have to pick them up and I'll help you."

"Eva did that. Eva did that. Bad Eva. No. No. No! Go to bed. Go to bed. Go to bed!"

Eva runs to the rug and slides underneath, crying.

"Daily news, daily news, bad Eva, bad, Eva. Spank Eva. Spank Eva." Eva beats her head with her fists. I pull her hands away from her head and hold them.

"I'm not going to let you hurt yourself. You don't have to punch or hit yourself. Eva's all right. I will not let you hurt yourself."

Eva screams. I have interrupted the ritual; I have broken the connection. She tries to yank my hair but I gently grip her wrists so that she can't hurt either of us.

"No, Eva, I won't let you hurt me and I won't let you hurt yourself. Come on, Eva. Eva is all right. Eva's not bad." I rock her body with the weight of my own body, while I hold the arms that want to scratch and claw. The thrashing subsides. Eva's body is limp again and she hums to herself. She has gone inside.

"Eva, Eva," I call, to find my way inside the walls, to wedge myself in somehow and bring her back. I shake her, I tickle her. I hold her and spin her.

"Bad Eva," she murmurs as in a trance, not talking to me or to anyone.

"No, Eva is not bad, not bad," I hear myself shout. "Eva and Miss Tina will pick everything up and it will be all right again. Eva is not bad."

"Not bad."

"That's right, Eva is not bad."

I gently pull Eva to her feet and move her as if she were a puppet, bending her arm down to pick up the toys. She helps me but her eyes are far away. All the toys, crayons and papers are picked up.

"Eva is a good girl." I hold her and rock her limp body in my arms.

May 11

In the bathroom Eva sings contentedly to herself. The faucet is turned on; I hear the dripping water.

"Come in, Miss Tina," a whisper.

Eva's voice, that's Eva calling to me. Mechanical, soft-sounding and far away; nevertheless it's Eva's voice.

Cautiously, I open the door not sure of what I'll find when I enter. The silence, the echolalia are both familiar to me. I've accustomed myself to them. I know their contours and their symbols. I'm now opening the door onto a new dimension. A voice seeking me out, asking me to come in is alien.

When I'm inside, Eva looks at me quickly and then bends her head down again. The humming starts up but nothing else. Did my mind contrive what I heard? No! I know I heard Eva speak to me.

"Here I am, Eva."

On the floor, I sit and wait and listen to the words not spoken. I believe I hear them.

'I let you in. Need to push you out again. Don't get too close or I will run. Don't get too close to me or I will hide. You will not find me. Find me, find me.'

The humming ceases and then starts up again. We sit in our separate silences, our insulated noises. I do not rush her. Soon the toilet flushes and Eva gets up.

"Miss Tina," she says softly a second time.

"Yes, Eva, here I am."

Eva turns the doorknob and opens the door. I wipe the dust off my black skirt and follow behind her.

A New Addition

May 12

Morning. I gulp down the remainder of my second coffee and wash my cup in the faculty sink before crossing the corridor to the main office to collect my keys from the key rack. The secretary motions me over to her desk.

"See that little girl?" Rita points to a skinny child with curly brown hair, who is standing by the bench, arms tightly braced against her chest. Her mouth pouts, tears spill down her face and she continually repeats the words, "No, no, no."

"Yes, who is she? She doesn't look familiar."

"She's your new charge."

"No warning? Did she just drop from heaven suddenly after all these weeks?"

"A school bus brought her here and will do so every day now."

Rita hands me a thick folder with papers on the new child, Patty Lewis, age eight. Language delayed and formerly attended school for the deaf.

"Attended what?" I hear myself say. But she's not deaf. Maybe there wasn't an appropriate placement for her or maybe they really believed she couldn't hear. Is this placement any more appropriate than before? I wonder.

"Patty, Hi, Patty," I smile when she turns to look at me.

"No!" she clenches her arms, locks her jaw firmly and looks away from me.

"Patty, I'm your teacher, Miss Tina. Are you ready to come up to the class with me? Come on, Patty. Let's go upstairs together, you and me."

"No!"

I put my hand on Patty's shoulder.

"No tuc me! No tuc me!" Patty cries.

I've never seen so many tears flow from one little girl all at once.

Rita watches us and silently crosses her fingers for luck. She shakes her head, the large gold hoop earrings swing from side to side, tapping her neck and she turns back to the pile of papers on her desk.

"Come on, Patty. Wouldn't you like to come up and play?"

"No! 'eave me 'lone. 'eave me!" Patty stamps her foot.

"Can I get some breakfast leftovers?" I implore Rita.

Rita telephones the lunchroom. A tall, lanky boy saunters in with a carton of milk and two raisin cookies. There is no string attached to them. No hook, no line, no sinker.

"Thanks." Willingly I take them from him.

"Patty, do you want a cookie and some milk?"

I am the wicked witch from the north. My house is made of gingerbread cookies and raisin bars and I eat little children for nourishment. I hold the booty out enticingly. The tears reverse themselves and wend miraculously back into Patty's head.

"Cu?" Patty questions.

"Yes, cookie. You can have a cookie. Patty can have a cookie. Come with me." I hold the cookie out and walk backwards through the office doorway.

"Come on, Patty."

Patty takes a step and then stops.

"No!" she wails. "No, No!"

In the hallway, Mr. Strong, the school counselor and my only ally, holds Eva by the hand as her head shakes fiercely from side to side. He sees me and smiles familiarly.

"Here you are," he says to me, letting go of Eva's limp hand. "I believe she's one of yours."

"Eva, here's Miss Tina. Have a good day, Eva and you too, Miss Tina," he winks encouragingly.

"Eva." Eva parrots her name and walks towards me.

"Thanks," I smile and take Eva's hand; she lets me without any resistance.

"Good morning, Eva." I greet her.

"Good morning, Eva."

"Eva, look, here's Patty. She's going to be with us." Patty watches Eva and me together.

"Patty, this is Eva. Eva and I are going up to our classroom together."

"No!" Patty screams.

"Eva, would you like a cookie?"

"Cookie?"

"Come on, Eva, walk with me. Here's the cookie."

I hold the cookie out to her and we walk. Eva's other hand is still loosely in mine.

"Come on, Patty, Let's go. Don't you want a cookie?"

Eva munches on the cookie while Patty hungrily watches its disappearance.

"Come on, Patty, here's the cookie. Let's go upstairs."

Patty walks several paces.

"Come on, Patty, we're almost there." I hold the cookie out to her. Patty grabs for it. She bites into the cookie, one morsel at a time. Then she stops in the middle of the hallway and won't budge.

"Come on, Patty."

"No." Patty hides the hand with the raisin cookie behind her and puts the other hand on her hip for emphasis. "No!"

Eva releases my hand and with a sidelong hop over to Patty, sniffs her. Eva runs away laughingly, her hands flutter up and down. I reach for Patty's hand but she pulls it back. Okay, I brace myself, take a deep breath and move closer. I reach out my hand again, this time touching my new student lightly on the shoulder. She kicks me in the shins, clutching the cookie proprietarily. Eva spins a short distance away from us.

"Ouch!"

"Come on, Eva," I call breathlessly. "Let's show Patty our classroom."

"Okay Patty, if you won't come upstairs now, that's just fine. We can all stay down here but our classroom is pretty. You might even like it."

A few teachers open their classroom doors to see what the commotion in the hallway is all about. One teacher whispers to another as they watch us. "What a shame. They are strange students, aren't they? And she can't even control them." My face reddens.

Patty throws herself to the floor, kicking and screaming. She pummels her hands against her ribs and thrashes her head from side to side. This isn't happening. I can't have this little girl risking self-injury in my care.

"Patty, now I'm going to count to three. One. I want you to stand up and walk with me and Eva to our classroom," I say calmly. If you don't come when I get to number three, I'm going to help you."

Patty doesn't move from the floor; she screams louder. Eva is whispering into her dancing fingers.

"Two."

Patty thrashes and bangs her fists on the floor. Wow, what a temper on her. She's not making this easy.

"Come on Patty. Let's get up from the floor and walk together."

Patty cracks her head down on the floor.

"Okay, three."

Now I must physically intervene, although I hoped that wouldn't be necessary, but when it comes to her safety, I'll make that decision every time. Bending down, I fasten Patty's arms to her sides and pick her up, holding her as close as her thrashing little body will allow. I can't leave Patty there; she's prone to hurt herself. She's hurt herself before, according to what I briefly managed to read in her file. I know I have to make time to review it later on. Right now, I have no choice but to put my own body between her and the hard floor. She kicks me.

Up the stairs, we climb. Patty's body feels like galvanized iron. Where Eva's is limp, Patty's is steel. Her heart pounds hard and quick; I can feel it against my chest.

More wallops to my thigh. Patty's foot comes down on me like a sledge hammer.

Somehow I manage to get the door open. Eva runs around us in circles, giggling and giggling. I wish I were amused, but I'm in need of a strong anodyne, wondering why, in this profession no one signs an affidavit consenting to masochism. Damn it, that kid can kick.

I set Patty down on the floor. She backs away from me, screaming and crying, beating the air as though it were my invisible effigy.

What a way to start the first day. Come out boxing in the ring. Poor Patty.

"You can stand there and calm down, Patty. When you're ready to come and join Eva and me on the carpet, you can. We're going to look at some pictures."

Cartons of milk and chocolate chip cookies sit temptingly on my desk waiting for snack-time. Amidst all the kicking and tears, I forgot to stash these edible goodies away for later.

Eva grabs the box of cookies from my desk, stuffs at least three in her mouth, and runs around holding the box with two overstuffed jaws.

Anyone for tennis?

"Eva, give the box of cookies back, please."

My request elicits a chain of giggles. Eva packs more in her mouth. She reaches into the box and takes the cookies, crunching them into crumbs onto the floor. Wonderful. A field day for ants and mice, waving their banners and jubilantly singing "The Marseillaise," crumbs bouncing jocularly along on their backs.

"Eva, give me the box of cookies. We won't have any left for our snack time."

Eva isn't disconcerted about that fact; only I am. She throws the cookie box up in the air and the paltry remains fly down upon her and the rug like a rainstorm. More giggles. Patty has not budged from her anchorage in the middle of the floor. Her arms are pressed across her upper torso like a rampart around her heart.

"Patty, don't you want to sit down? I'll show you where your desk is. See here," I gesticulate, "Here's where Patty sits. This is Patty's desk."

"No, go 'way, go 'way."

Even more tears. I have tapped the reservoir with my words.

Armed with scissors, paper and paste, I retreat to the rug. Eva watches me thumb through the magazines and saunters over. She sits down on our blanket of crumbs and waves her arms.

"Look at the little boy, Eva. Isn't he cute?" I draw out the word liltingly. Eva laughs.

"Cute," she repeats.

"Yes, he's so-oo-oo cute. Shall we cut out the little boy, Eva?"

I cut the picture while Eva leans into my arm.

"Do you want to paste the picture, Eva?"

"Paste the picture."

"Here, here is the paste, let's put some paste on the paper with the stick so we don't get our fingers full of paste."

I guide Eva's hand from the jar of paste to the paper. Her grasp on the stick lacks strength. When the paste covers the back of the picture, Eva takes the cute little boy and slaps him crookedly on another blue paper.

"So-oo-oo-oo cute," Eva mimics the rise and fall of my voice.

"Yes, he is so-oo-oo cute." I pretend to kiss the little boy. Eva smiles and looks at me.

I am a comic, a clown, a buffoon. My movements and words are focused on the moment of another's laughter, another's response. The antics I perform are to secure Eva here with me, and to make her laugh.

Rigid is the only word I can find to describe Patty. How can a person stay fixed on one point with her entire body for three quarters of an hour? There are no bolts; I've already checked that out. She just stands there, rooted and forlorn.

I put on the familiar music which Eva and I dance to now. Eva loves it. It gives me an opportunity to make physical contact with Eva by ushering her through the movements.

"Make yourself small," the voices sing out the instructions. I stoop low and gently pull Eva down with me. "Make yourself tall." I lift us up while raising Eva's hands high in the air.

When the lunches come, Eva and I wash our hands together at the sink. I wet her face with my watery hand and she licks my hand playfully. If Patty has moved, I missed it.

"Patty, it's time to eat lunch. Wouldn't you like to eat lunch with Eva and Miss Tina? Come on, let's wash up. Here are the lunches. Come to the table with us."

"No, 'eave me wone, 'eave me wone."

Eva and I sit together at the table now. Eva opens her milk but can't unwrap the plastic her straw is in. She holds her hand out to me.

"What do you want me to do, Eva?"

Silence.

"Do you want me to open this for you?"

"Open."

Patty watches us. She looks at Eva as Eva bites into the hamburger. When I turn around to look at Patty, her head twists the other way.

"Patty, don't you want to eat?"

Patty doesn't answer. In my mind is a vision of an already thin little girl growing skinnier and skinnier. Emaciated. So this is what they do in special-needs classes. They starve the children into obedience. Wonderful. I swallow the dried-out hamburger meat and muse over the cost of my lawyer's fees.

Patty walks over to the window and starts to cry again. "Bussie ca bac," she sobs. "Bussie ca bac."

"The bus is coming back, Patty. The bus will come back to take you home. Don't worry, the bus will be back."

My words do not console. Patty won't eat, won't leave the windowsill, seat of her wanderlust; she waits for the bus to take her home again. Hours in front of the window—crying and watching—all on an empty stomach. Finally Patty's bus arrives.

"Patty, your bus is here. Your bus has come to take you home. See."
I go to the window and point to the yellow bus waiting in front of the
school. "See, there's your bus. Your bus is ready to take you home."

"Come on, Eva," I call to Eva who is lying on her back, knees
up, watching her fingers dance in front of her. "Let's walk Patty
downstairs so she can catch her bus."

At first Patty doesn't want to go. Must we repeat this morning's
performance?

"Your bus is here," I say brightly, all smiles. "See, your bus?"

She follows me out the door very slowly. Her feet have weights attached to them. Suppose I have lied to her and that's not her bus at all?

Eva runs ahead and hops down the stairs. I'm next. Patty holds
onto the railing and guardedly walks down one step per minute. I
calculate that at this rate we will reach the bottom in half an hour.

"Come on, hurry up, your bus is here, your bus is here," I singsong. "Patty's bus is here."

Eva disappears through the doors and I speed up my pace. I watch
Eva sailing into the office. Patty emerges through the doors, sees her
bus driver and smiles. The first smile I have seen in over six hours.

"See, Patty, your bus is here to take you home."

Patty leaps past me and sprints out the door of the school with
the bus driver.

"Bye, Patty," I call to no one in particular. No one in particular
answers.

Now to retrieve Eva. In the office Eva collects all the visible
papers: notices for teachers, notes to parents, anything that is paper-
like with writing on it. Her hands are full. The secretaries look at me
beseechingly. Eva surveys Rita's desk for more papers to add to her
already overfull arms.

"Eva, you can't have these, you must give them back."

"No, no!" Eva screams and rushes out of the office. Everyone in
the hallway turns around to hear Eva wailing at the top of her lungs.

"Give them back, Eva. Let's give them back to the secretaries.
They need them to do their work. Give them back."

"No back, no back!" Eva spits on the floor. She sees the driver and runs in the opposite direction.

"No home, no home, no back, no back. Bad Eva, bad Eva!" Her screams are more like warrior cries, shrill and deadly. Teachers emerge from their rooms to see what the commotion is. I hear a door slam hard and then another.

Eva snorts out all the mucus stored in her nose, thinking this disgusting display will keep everyone at bay. She starts to rip the pages venomously. Just in time, I reach her. I take the papers; Eva's fingers are curled ready to scratch at me.

"That's okay, Eva, I have the papers now. Eva's not bad. We'll give the papers back and see if the secretaries will let Eva keep one to take home." All this as soothingly as I can, with chicken wire tearing the insides of my stomach lining. We finally get to the office. Eva cries as though she's been unmercifully beaten. I hold her around the shoulders, coo to her, and repeat the same words over and over. Hopefully she hears them. Eva's voice is rasping; she is gasping for breath. I take a tissue and wipe her face and her nose. With another tissue I wipe the sweat from her forehead.

"Eva, everything is all right. Let's see if we can have a paper to take home." Now my eyes implore Rita.

"Here, Eva," Rita says, meeting my gaze, "you can take this one home." Rita holds out a week-old teacher's bulletin. Eva looks at the paper and reaches for it.

"Let's go, Eva, you can take the paper home in the bus."

"No bus, no home!"

Just then the school bus aide downstages.

"Come on, Eva, let's go now, the bus driver is waiting to take everyone home and we're already late," the matron's voice is impatient.

"No! No! No!"

"Eva, come on, it's time to go home," I repeat.

The aide has one arm and I'm holding onto the other while Eva writhes and kicks.

"Eva, your mommy is waiting for you. You can show her the paper you brought for her."

"Paper?"

"Yes, Eva, the paper."

Eva sniffles, still writhing, yet somehow, due to our guiding arms, glides miraculously to the bus.

"Goodbye, Eva." I kiss her cheek.

"No home, no home!" she screams inside the bus. Her face is pressed against the window; her cries can be heard up to the third floor of the school. The bus driver shakes his head and drives off.

I walk back past the office and stop at the doorway for a friendly face.

"Rita, would you please let the janitor know that my classroom needs vacuuming? Cookie crumbs are sprinkled everywhere."

"Sure thing, and what are you going to do this evening?" Rita inquires.

"After banging my head against the wall, I'm going to say over and over, that I'm a good person, until it finally sinks in." We both laugh and I realize that I have another school ally.

"I think you have the right idea, Tina. Don't take all this too seriously and don't let this place get to you. Go easy on yourself or you'll go crazy. Believe me, I know. I've seen that happen a few times in this job, no kidding! And your challenge is over the top. Do something relaxing and get your mind off of work."

We both smile. Rita is so right and I can't agree more. Martinis, anyone? Make mine very, very dry.

May 15

I wait outside the school building for my class of two. I watch while children flood from the many buses that arrive from all over the district. Some are rowdy and tumbling from the doors, school-bags thrust over their shoulders as they shout and run after their friends. Others are quieter and more somber at the start of the school day, sleep scarcely brushed from their eyes, the taste of breakfast still on their lips, yawns still lurking at the backs of their mouths.

Patty's bus arrives but Patty isn't on it.

"What happened? Where is Patty?" I ask the bus driver.

"When I got to her house I honked and waited. No one came to the door. I got out and knocked but if anybody was in there, nobody came. Sure looked real quiet, like they was sleeping or something. I'm guessing nobody was home."

"Guess not. Thanks."

So it's just Eva and me again—for today at least. Hopefully, the school administration will get to the bottom of Patty's no-show.

As for Eva, I feel that now's the time to introduce more academics. She can focus on activities and there's bonding between us. I believe our exchange is strong enough to try some active learning without risking further alienation from me and without any setback to Eva's progress. When Eva comes I greet her as I do every morning.

"Hi, Eva."

"Hi, Miss Tina." This is the very first morning in all our months together she has said good morning and used my name. No echolalia, no silence, but a genuine hello! Mark this on the calendar. I smile a deep, deep smile that I can feel coursing right through the very center of me. I feel love for this little girl and also pride for her accomplishments.

I begin to appreciate the little spurts of progress and recognize that they are actually giant leaps. Small giant leaps that move us forward into new ventures of language, learning, and speaking. This is the way they happen—slowly, painstakingly, in tune with some inner timetable. I accept them, examine them, and nourish them. Eva is learning and talking more; maybe not all the time but right now, we have begun. We have turned a new corner and it's wonderful.

"Eva, you said hello to me. Hurray!" In my exuberance, I hug her. She doesn't shrink away from me, but feels warm, present. We walk upstairs together.

"Patty's not coming today. She's at home."

"Home."

"Yes, so you and I are going to play with the letter puzzle together and learn the letters."

"Letters."

"A-B-C-D-E-F-G-H-I-J-K" I sing the alphabet song to Eva, while we hold hands and I swing our arms.

We sit on the rug with the puzzle box. The letters and pictures fit together.

" 'A' is for Apple," I call them as we put them together. We complete the puzzle once, and Eva wants to do it again. She takes the puzzle apart.

" 'A' is for Apple," Eva says. " 'B' is for Boat."

She names every letter, save for three. She remembers everything with no rehearsal and no prompting. Eva does the letter puzzle five times and now has all the letters correct. We finish and I pick Eva up and spin her around. Eva laughs. Gently, I lower Eva down onto the rug again and sit a little away from her.

"Roll to me," I call, moving her body along the rug in a rolling motion.

"Roll to me."

Eva rolls her body with assistance from me. When she gets close I roll her away. Eva waits.

"Roll to me," I chant again. "Roll to me."

Eva rolls her body, and laughs in anticipation of what will happen when she reaches her destination. I roll her away and the giggles burst like bubbles onto the rug. Again Eva waits. I say nothing. She waits and waits, not moving her body, her head cocked for the sound she listens for. No voice.

"Roll to—." Eva begins, wanting me to complete the lilting phrase.

"Me." I say. That word sets Eva's body into motion. She is next to me. We giggle and I gently roll her away again.

"Roll to—." I imitate Eva.

"Me," she says. This time when Eva rolls to me I tickle her. Eva giggles and rolls away.

"Roll to—." Now it's her turn.

"Me," I say.

May 16

Two whole days and no Patty. We'll pretend that whole episode never happened. She never came to school battling to go home again. It was a mirage, something I invented for comic relief. Sometimes I'm astounded by the strangeness of the relationships between the children and me and by the intensity of our meetings. The intensity is so profound and then, just like that, a child is gone as if the meetings never happened. Yet they did happen.

Patty's phone is disconnected and has been for several months, so the only way to make contact is in person. The social worker from our district and I confer. She tells me that she made a visit to the house but no one was home. When further inquiries were made, the social worker was informed that the family had moved.

A family packs itself up and vanishes stealthily into the night, into their caravan like gypsies. One mother and three children are gone leaving no trace. No one, including the neighbors, knows anything of their whereabouts. I tell Eva that Patty's not here and will continue to do so until Patty's name no longer surfaces. I don't imagine that this will take too long. Patty was a classmate for such a short time and there wasn't really any bonding between the two of them.

Eva recognizes and identifies all the letters of the alphabet. Her ability to recall is uncanny. Learning takes place now with such rapidity. Today we concentrated on the letter sounds. Eva works longer at each activity now; the interest is there. Eva wants to learn; she wants to know. As if she yearns for all the pieces of the world's puzzle to cohere, to create order out of disorder. The symbols of my world are becoming more familiar and desirable the more she learns.

"'C' is for cat, 'C' is for cake, 'C' is for crayon, 'C' is for coke,"

Eva skips around reciting to herself. She has plugged into a new tape recording, "The World of Letters, Sounds and Names." Her day is composed of naming and asking over and over, "What is this, what is this?"

"This is a flower; this is an elephant. That is a farmhouse and that is a monkey." I name everything Eva wants to know about. Her world is enlarging and the categories are expanding. We have covered years in just days. Something inside of Eva opens like the Morning Glory when touched by the sun. Suddenly ash is transformed into flame. The classroom feels lighter and brighter as Eva engages more and more with the world outside herself. Her new energy is intoxicating and it fills the room. We look at all sorts of pictures. There is impatience, such urgency in her to find out the different flavors of learning she has yet to taste and sample.

Eva loves to draw pictures on the chalkboard. I take out large kaleidoscope pieces of colored chalk and Eva fills up the board with her imagination.

"Eva's house," she points to a picture she has drawn. "Eva lives here. And mommy and Ronnie and Rodney."

"Who are Ronnie and Rodney?"

"Brothers."

"Eva's brothers?"

"Eva's brothers. Ronnie and Rodney."

"Eva has two brothers and one mommy and daddy. Eva has a family," I tell her.

"Family, family," Eva repeats softly to herself and inside her dancing fingers, memorizing the new word as she tries to make sense of it.

May 17

Eva is learning how to spell! I would never have believed it possible. A little girl who would not talk is learning and spelling words as fast as she can. Her appetite for learning is insatiable. Dog, Eva,

Miss Tina, school, bus driver, sun, smile, giggle, leg, arm, brother, mother, toy, run! Everything she hears she wants spelled. Eva retains it all, not just for a day. Once it's a part of her memory, she doesn't forget. If I ever doubted her intelligence or misjudged her ability to take everything in while seemingly tuning everything out, I was wrong. Deep down I knew that there was more here—more to Eva than what was visible. What a mind and what a glow to her when she can focus and wants to learn.

Yet, despite all this job demands of me, I wouldn't do anything differently. The work I do gets me fired up and out of the house, with service in my heart and a sense of responsibility that is so real and important. Never, ever boring or repetitive, each day is fresh and filled with new surprises. This is the magic that motivates me again and again. Everything revolves around the relationships here, even the learning. I know that Eva needed to trust me and feel comfortable before she was ready to learn and experiment with non-familiar realms. Now those foreign places have become ones that she welcomes into her life with an eagerness that is akin to that of a toddler who seeks to explore a brand new world.

I've learned as much from Eva in these past few months as she has learned from me. She has taught me about myself, about the significance of trust between a student and teacher and about the silent and dancing place within my own heart. Thank you Eva, my little spelling genius!

May 18

More carpet time. Eva and I are looking at pictures in a magazine.
"People," Eva points to the page.
"That's right, Eva, they are people."
"Spell people?" Eva says.
"P-e-o-p-l-e: people."
Eva spells it for herself.
"Cut," she tells me. With my help, Eva cuts the picture.

"Paste," she suggests.

Eva spreads the paste by herself and stares at the picture she has cut and pasted. She sniffs it and then hugs the picture to her chest.

"I like people," Eva says to me.

"I know you do, and I like Eva." I smile and we rub noses.

May 19

Guess who has returned, dressed in a red and white polka-dot suit, with a new home address and a brand new bus driver?

"Hi, Patty," I greet her.

"No," she says again. It's as if we never left off.

"Are you ready to go upstairs with Eva and Miss Tina?" I ask.

"No," she stamps her foot.

Did I expect anything different?

"Oh well, bye Patty!" I turn as if to leave.

"No," Patty pouts.

"No?" I ask.

"No," she says.

"No!" I exaggerate the sound of it. Patty laughs and then, re-membering that she's not supposed to cooperate and enjoy this, she frowns and turns away.

"No, no, no!" she voices a melody of refusal.

"No, no, no," I say in imitation; simultaneously I stamp my feet.

Patty stops and watches her mirror-self. I turn away and walk upstairs. Patty follows while she pretends to tiptoe through a field of dandelions, and examines each wild flower in the floor. I slow down, in case she's forgotten the winding path to our room. Enough distance ahead, she can't see me watch her. I have become a master of games and intrigue. Patty's in no hurry. Like a thief, she glances in all directions to ensure that no one lurks on the stairwell to cap-ture her. I wait at the top of the stairs. She climbs to the summit, our little mountaineer, and sees me.

"No, no!" she screams. Then she looks down and beholds the

view. From the top of the mountain everything below looks far off and treacherous. Patty opts for the mountaintop. She follows me to the door which I leave open, and stands midway between earth and heaven. Both lack appeal. I see no reason to coerce Patty further. She has come far. What matters is that she's there and visible. I can monitor her from my post and make sure she's not in harm's way.

The phone rings. The bus aide is downstairs with a note from Eva's mother. Will I please come down and pick it up? Sure, just fly in a chairlift and Patty and I will glide down to the office as easily as we went up.

"Can you send it up with a messenger, please, Rita? I have my hands tied."

"You don't mean to tell me that little lightweight has you in knots?" Rita chuckles.

"You know, Rita, I think you've missed your calling. Have you ever considered becoming a comedienne?"

"Only in my wildest dreams. I'll send it up by messenger."

"Thanks."

Patty examines the hair, the hair follicles, and counts (if she can count) the pores on her arms and hands. The note arrives from Mrs. Turner.

"Dear Miss Randolph,

"Please excuse Eva. She has the mumps."

Poor little chipmunk.

I open a carton of milk and the newly purchased box of cookies. Patty peers around the door and into the classroom. I think children have an electronic radar device in their noses which immediately picks up the scent of anything remotely sweet and edible.

"Patty, would you like some milk and cookies?"

"Huh?"

Oh no, here we are again, not the dumb blonde routine.

"Milk and cookies," I raise my voice.

"Huh?"

"Milk and cookies, milk and cookies, how would you like some milk and cookies?" I singsong. Maybe it's my voice, maybe I've surprised her; Patty smiles.

"You want a cookie?"

Patty's hand ventures out. Everything else is stationary. I put a cookie in her hand and walk away. Leave a trail of crumbs to light up the path to the good witch's house, that way the little angel will know which way to come. Unethical, maybe — administering cookies as placation, yet it works. Patty needs to feel at home and safe and, besides, it's almost recess so I feel justified.

Patty's still standing outside the classroom door, her fingers twist and play with the red polka-dot fabric of her dress and she leans into the door frame as if it could conceal her.

"Cu?"

"You can have another cookie in the classroom, Patty."

"Cu."

"Yes, cookies are tasty. You can have another one when you come in the classroom and then, when the morning is over and you've done some work, then we can have a cookie again at lunchtime."

I hold out my hand to invite her in. My hand is tired and Patty will not cross the imaginary line into enemy territory.

"Here, Patty. Look, here are the cookies." I hold the box of cookies to show her.

"I'm going to put these over on the shelf, see, over here. When you come in the classroom, you can have another cookie. Then we'll take them down and eat one at lunchtime. Look, see."

I walk over to the wall across from the classroom door and place the box on the shelf.

Patty cautiously steps across the threshold and into our classroom. Her eyes are riveted to the box of cookies on the opposite side of the room. If she averts her eyes, the cookies might mysteriously disappear.

"Thanks for coming into the classroom, Patty. You can have a cookie now."

I hand Patty her second morning snack.

She grips the cookie and runs to her post at the window.

"C'mon busie," Patty pleads.

"C'mon busie," I repeat.

"C'mon."

"Come on busie, c'mon," I say imitating her inflection.

Patty finds my mimicry amusing. She giggles. The "busie" game continues forever. Patty will not eat lunch but does eat her lunchtime cookie. Nor will she play with anything. She sits and watches the traffic ride past the window waiting for the moment when she can go home again. I read a story aloud to Patty, but she never acknowledges my words.

May 20

I lie in bed on my back with my head raised up on several of the pillows and cushions that are scattered across the bed. The sheets are a little sweaty and it takes all my energy to reach for the phone.

"Hi Rita, this is Tina," I say, projecting my weary voice to be heard.

"Hi. What can I do for you, this rainy morning?"

"I want you to know something that I've just discovered."

"What could that be?"

"I never had the mumps when I was a child."

"Well, that's just wonderful. Now what's that supposed to mean in the here and now?" There's a pause, followed by an "Oh, no! You don't mean…"

"Yes, I mean just that. I look like a frog. That is, all except for the color."

"What are we going to do?"

"One comforting thought — Eva won't be there, she's still home with the mumps, but what about Patty?"

"I don't know. Maybe we can head them off at the pass. I'll call you back."

A little later, while I'm in the midst of spooning strawberry yogurt down my tender throat, Rita calls.

"Well, you're lucky. Patty isn't coming today. The principal is fit to be tied. He called down to district headquarters and bawled out anyone he could find connected with this program. 'Why isn't there a substitute to cover the class in case of illness?' etc. etc. At this rate he'll be gray by the end of the day, I tell you."

"But, Rita, Mr. Donahue doesn't have any hair."

"His skull will turn gray then. Listen, I can't talk, I've got a zillion things to do, you know how it is and, besides, even the walls have ears in this place. Get well and don't read too many romantic novels."

"I don't have any. What are they going to do about tomorrow and the next day?"

"It's okay, we've a reprieve. Patty won't be back until next week nor will your Eva. But after that we can't promise, so no more absence requests, please. Feel better. Bye dear."

"Thanks, Rita. Bye."

Feeling lonely and sorry for myself and in need of some TLC, I dial my mother. Not that I expected anyone to be home on a weekday morning.

"Mom, it's your other daughter. When you get in, please call me." I always tease mom although she's never confused my voice with my sister's. "Your voices are as distinctive as your personalities," she always says.

May 24

"Hi, Eva."

"Hi, Miss Tina. I had mumps."

"I had the mumps, too."

I puff my cheeks out and she laughs. Eva and I go upstairs and make words with the magnetic board. Eva has difficulty writing out the words by hand. It's a frustrating process for her, which ends up in paper-ripping, pencil-smashing, and a fusillade of tears. I don't want to ruin her pleasure with letters and spelling. Nor douse her interest in learning and discovery when she's so ready to absorb more. So we create words with moveable letters—for now.

The Journey Out of the Deep

May 27

Eva has started to make progress with the pen and can now write her name, slowly and with arduous concentration.

"Look," Eva points to the scrawl as though it were her first masterpiece.

"Eva, it's beautiful!"

We trace letters. Eva practices for over an hour. Patty's bus is late, and when it does arrive, Patty emerges, all jumps and hops.

"Hi Patty."

"Hi," she responds. Will wonders never cease? We are beginning. Patty is still adamant about doing anything but window gazing.

Today she eats lunch, where else but in front of the window. Eva rushes over to Patty and sniffs her and the lunch. Patty whines, bending over her food to conceal it from Eva and her voracious appetite.

May 30

Patty and Eva chase each other around the room. They have acknowledged each other's existence and can both live in the territory together. I'll allow the chasing interaction briefly because it's how they're beginning to relate to each other. A union is formed: Patty and Eva against Miss Tina. Patty distrusts me and feels safer as Eva's shadow. Eva doesn't make contact with anyone for long, tires of the game and sits alone shuffling letter cards in her hands.

June 3

When I turn to the calendar, I realize we're already in the last lap. We've come all this distance; soon summer vacation will predicate our separation. I must prepare Eva for this separation and for the change in routine that will follow; I'll need to prepare myself too.

Patty hasn't been here enough to feel drawn into the nexus of trust and caring. She's a visitor who stops in just long enough to say hello and then disappears for a week or so. Momma has moved again, packing and unpacking her clan. Every time she changes her address, a new bus route has to be found, which takes time.

As for Eva, she has given birth to herself here. For Eva, this place tastes, smells and feels like home. She has learned to venture forth one step at a time, and I have been there to catch her. Her discovery of this world has had the face of pleasure, not only the tempest.

And me? I'm changed. I've been opened by a little girl. Mother, teacher, therapist, friend—they have not been masks, but I have worn them. Eva's world doesn't baffle me any longer. I am stronger. Eva is stronger. The voices can be reckoned with. When she goes inside, I have faith that she will come back out again.

June 7

"Eva, soon summer will be here and this school will be closed."
"Closed?"
"Yes, all the children won't come back until September. No one will be here. I won't be here either. I'll be home."
"Home."
"Yes, I'll work in my garden at home, read and relax. You'll be home too with your family."
"Family."
"Yes, you'll be home with your brothers and your mom and your dad. No school for us until September."

"No school."

"That's right. School will be closed."

"Eva?"

"Eva will be home for the summer. When school starts again, Eva will be back, and Miss Tina will be back, too."

"Eva be back?"

"Yes, Eva will be back, and Miss Tina will be back."

"Patty?"

"Hopefully, Patty will come back with us and other children."

"Children?"

"We'll have more children in our class."

"More children, and Eva and Miss Tina and Patty?"

"Yes, we'll all be here again when summer's over."

June 10

I circle the dates on the calendar: when school will be closed and when it will open again. Rituals of endings are as important as beginnings. We mark off the days in blue slanted lines. Each morning we count the remaining days till the end of the school year.

Patty is with us today. We all walk upstairs together. Patty eats lunch with us at the table as if it's the most natural thing in the world, although it feels like an eternity to have come this far. Yet, Patty's isolation from us is now in the past. Eating lunch with us tells me that she's ready to join in and be part of the class and the circle of trust. This is her way to relate and cooperate. Not that there won't be more challenges for her and for all of us. Challenges are easier to face when there's fellowship and support. After slurping her dessert, Patty grins at us, peach juice drips down the sides of her mouth. I have not spoken to her about table manners — yet.

"Hi," she says.

'Hi' is better than 'No.' It's a confirmation of us and herself, rather than a denial or a rejection. A limited vocabulary, one word is all inclusive.

"Hi," I return the bestowal and Eva laughs.

June 11

Patty grips a pocketbook she brought from home with all the tenacity of a miser. "Mine," she doesn't neglect to point out to all who come within five feet of her property.

"Yes, it's Patty's." I shake my head agreeably. Patty approves my acquiescence to her rights of possession. However, she won't release the purse. When she sits down to eat, it's tucked under her free arm. When she plays in the sandbox, it rests in her lap. An appendage, her treasure she needs to hide and guard. Only Eva dares to challenge its ownership.

"I want to see," Eva cries, when Patty shoves Eva away from her. Eva sniffs the pocketbook and, to my surprise, Patty wallops her with the strength of a tigress.

"No, mine. No!"

"I want to see. Want to see," Eva repeats.

"Mine, don't tuc."

Eva circles around Patty but is afraid of reprisal if she gets too near. A sneak attack from behind as Eva tries to grab the purse away. Patty wails. Before I can intervene to stop them, Patty leaps. Two belts to Eva's leg with Patty's shoe and Eva rushes away angrily, not ready to battle the forces of physical power. Her fingers dance nervously in front of her face, while Eva hums to herself, sheltered under her umbrella of forgetting.

"Mine, mine, mine," Patty mumbles. Her voice is hoarse, she doesn't stop the recording.

"Mine, mine, mine," she chants for the remaining hour.

June 12

Eva hides in the closet.

"Come in, Patty," she calls out.

Yesterday's battle is buried. Patty is alone, her purse left at home. In the closet, they play together. Ten minutes. Something important is happening. The circle is widening to include Patty. I watch silently, nothing but a breathing presence while this magic is happening. These two little girls are opening to each other; including each other in their games and their separate realities like all children.

June 16

No Patty. Eva and I go to the playground. The air is balmy as we press ourselves beyond the confines of our classroom and the school. I'm glad for the chance to be outside with Eva and wonder why I haven't done this sooner. I realize it only feels natural today because of where we are right now. Eva has come so far and there's an established bond and code of understanding between us now. Before this, the risk of her getting hurt on the swings or of undoing the work we had already done was too great. It wasn't the right time and now it is.

When Eva sees the swing, she lets go of my hand, prancing ahead. One jump and Eva is in the seat.

"Push Eva."

As the swing soars upward, Eva closes her eyes and leans her head back.

"Do you want to go up high?"

"High. Up."

"Eva is swinging. High, up, up, up high. Up in the sky," I sing as I push the swing while Eva's legs reach out and up, eager to climb up and wanting to fly.

"High, higher."

She isn't afraid! The swing slows down, swaying from side to side as Eva's feet brush the earth acting as brakes. Eva hops off and runs into my arms.

"I love you," Eva whispers. The monotone isn't gone from her voice; the words are muffled against my chest, but the meaning of those words has never been clearer.

"I love you too," I whisper.

June 19

This is the start of the last week of school with three days left before Eva and I part for the summer. Will everything she's learned remain with her when she returns in September? Endings and good-byes aren't easy and they've never been simple for me. From what I've learned about Eva and her difficulty to form attachments to people, this separation won't be easy for her either. Despite how hard and how long it took, a relationship between us was molded. I only hope that the summer vacation won't undo the bond between us and all the academic progress we've made.

I know next year will be very different. Eva and I won't have the luxury to experience each other the same way we do now. More children, at least three more I know about. Will Eva be able to share me with the others? Is there enough of me to nurture them all with some left over for myself? I still have many questions and so much to digest about the progress we've made this year. The vacation will be a good opportunity for a little reflection—not to mention some well-needed R and R! I've forgotten what a day devoted exclusively to me feels like. Even my weekends are filled with Eva and Patty—their voices, their worlds and their experiences. 'Switching off' is not a habit that comes naturally in this job. However, leaving the work behind is an essential habit I must cultivate for my own sanity and peace of mind.

June 21

"Eva, this is our last day together. See, all the school days on the calendar are marked in blue? There aren't any school days left. School closes and we'll have to wait to come back here."

"Come back."

"Yes, we will come back and see each other and Patty and the new children. We'll all be here after vacation."

"No more school?"

"No more school. For a long time: the rest of June, July and August, two whole months. In September, school will start again. We'll say hello and work and play together just like now."

"No school, no school," she speaks to her fingers. "Miss Tina says no school."

The bus driver is waiting outside and beams at me.

"Well you made it," he wipes his balding head with his handkerchief, "my hat is off to you." He nods in my direction.

"Thanks."

"Eva," I bend down so we're at eye level. "Have a very nice summer and learn lots of new words. I'll see you after vacation, and Eva," I hug her very close to me; "I will miss you."

Eva breaks away, avoiding my eyes and flies up the bus steps. After the bus pulls out, I stand there on the curb where we first met.

New Beginnings

June 25

The long summer vacation is both a blessing and a curse. Patterns and rhythms are so polarized for a teacher: from glaring, full-speed, non-stop to two gentle months of 'rest' and 'downtime'. Adjusting to this pace isn't easy. The first couple of weeks brim with mixed emotions of sadness and relief—not to mention an exhaustion that hits me like a truck! I give into the fatigue, get up later than usual, and bask in my well-deserved laziness for a short time until my energy returns. I slip into a summer of friends and ease knowing my civilian life will be short-lived.

August 15

I begin to think about school once again. What new projects and learning games can I introduce into the curriculum to make learning irresistible? Although I've reviewed the individual educational programs of the new students, called IEP's, meeting and teaching them personally are so different from what I glean from the paper work. Soon enough, I'll know more.

September 1

Summer is ending. Although I feel refreshed and rejuvenated from the time off, I also experienced some loneliness during these weeks, a loneliness that comes from parting with a loved one. I learned to love a little person throughout the triumph and the terror, in war and peacetime, to love one who is not my flesh and blood, but is a stranger. Sometimes I felt her pain as my own, but then the victories were mine, also. A swelling pride I shared in the moment when Eva said "Yes" to this life. Wanting to know more and more of this world because it wasn't only a hostile battleground; there was love in it: love that was genuine, and not cellophane-wrapped like a piece of candy.

My mind has started to wander. I feel a growing restlessness and crave a faster-paced routine and some more responsibility. I start to count the days until I can resume my duties and find myself thinking about Eva and Patty and the other children I haven't even met. I prepare some work for the children I do know, planning programs based on what I know of them so far and the progress they've made. I also write down lessons and learning activities that I believe will work well for the new children. Brainstorming games and ideas to help me—things I can pull out of my sleeve when we are all together and looking at each other tentatively in those first few days. Preparation in teaching, I've learned, is really necessary and I enjoy doing it. Nights are cooler now and autumn is making her early return. What colors will she bring me in the faces of my children?

September 6

And so we begin again. This time with an expected full house: Eva and I. Patty, Ricardo, Martin, and Kaye, my teacher's aide. That's the preliminary lineup. The room seemed so large last year; I had trouble crossing the expanse to Eva. Now that the spaces are rapidly filling up, the room feels smaller. My attention is to be divided among four children with two more on the way in the coming weeks. A program begun one-on-one has burgeoned into a real class with real people. A language therapist is soon to appear.

Kaye and I greet each other formally, guardedly. Are we so different from the children?

We don't talk much; we have an entire year to do that. Today I come back and revisit the times spent here in this space. The walls are silent; there is no evidence of Eva's former rage. The rug has been shampooed and vacuumed; antiseptically smoothing away memories of Eva's rocking and head-banging. There are no voices. The ghosts have vanished. I want the room to be bright and airy to dissolve any lingering scent of fear and denial here.

September 9

The children arrive in throngs and pairs and solo, jabbering and sharing their vacation stories in short bites. Is there always so much excitement and energy generated on this day? I can feel the buzz of new beginnings, high hopes and awakened energy in myself and all around me. The halls are electric; the students clean and radiant.

Outside my door stand a mother and a muscular boy wearing a blue and black checkered shirt and blue jeans. There is something polished and clean about his clothes, his neatly pressed brown trousers, and the way he carries himself. Mother is whispering and looks a little piqued around the soft edges of her face. She bends over him, a gesture of compliance rather than tyranny.

"Now, Martin, I wish you wouldn't carry on so. You know that you like school once you get used to it. It's no use to behave the way you are. Martin, you have to go to school. Your father will be furious. Come on, Martin. Let's go inside, now."

"No, I'm not going inside of this room. She looks awful and I'll bet she beats children for raising their hands. A monster, I'm not going to be in the same room as a monster. Ugh. I think I'm going to be sick."

Dry retching outside my doorway; I decide to intercede.

"Hello, may I help you?"

"Yes. This is Martin and I'm Mrs. Selby."

"I'm so glad to meet you, Mrs. Selby. Hello, Martin, how are you?"

Martin assumes a nonchalant pose, worthy of a nobleman in a

classical painting. Nose lifted in the air, arms across his chest, his right foot impatiently taps at 99 beats per minute.

"I'm Miss Tina Randolph. I'll be Martin's teacher this year. I've been expecting you, Martin."

"Miss Tina Randolph," he mimics my name.

"Miss Randolph, where are the other children? Martin comes from a school where he was expected to do advanced academic work. I wouldn't want him to fall behind. You know Martin is not a problem once you understand how to handle him. Isn't that right, Martin?"

"Humph."

"I'm sure that's true, Mrs. Selby, and I assure you, every child will be working up to his own potential. I've reviewed Martin's IEP, the individualized education program sent over from his former school to familiarize myself with Martin's academic levels and with the prescribed instruction. Please, Mrs. Selby, you have nothing to worry about. I'm sure Martin will do well here. And, I always welcome input from the parents to help me understand each child's unique needs and interests. Please feel free to contact me by phone. Or if it's easier, Mrs. Selby, just send a note along with Martin."

"I'm glad to hear that." Mrs. Selby looks dubious. Martin squeezes his arms against his stomach and moans but doesn't neglect to slick down his jet black hair with his fingers.

"What is it, Martin? What's wrong?"

"I think it's my appendix."

"Maybe if you come inside and sit down, the pain will go away," I suggest.

Martin telegraphs daggers with his charcoal eyes.

"I have to go soon. A neighbor's waiting for me in the car. You know, I hope they get this bus route straightened out soon. I can't bring him every day. I don't drive and it means imposing on other people."

"Yes, I understand how inconvenient that can be. If you have to go now, that's all right. Let's arrange to meet very soon to discuss any concerns you may have and to review Martin's school program.

If it's okay with you, I'll call you early next week to arrange for a time to meet together."

"Yes, fine. Are you sure that he'll be all right? Martin, is your stomach any better?"

"I think it's much worse." His voice has more cramping in it than I believe his stomach to have.

"He'll be just fine." I stare levelly at Martin. He's prolonging this as long as he can. Oh, the language of the eyes.

"Well, I hate to leave him if he feels…"

"There's a very competent school nurse here. If there is something wrong, he'll be well taken care of. I think it's just the excitement of a new school and the first day."

"Well, maybe you're right. I don't like taking any chances with his health. You know Martin had scarlet fever when he was a year old and it affected his heart."

The smirk glistening in his dark eyes is unmistakable.

"He'll be fine, Mrs. Selby, just fine."

"Bye, now, Martin. If your stomach is upset, don't eat the lunch I've made you. Bring it home."

Martin's face is stony and he dismissively turns his back to her. Mrs. Selby shrugs embarrassedly and walks away.

"Goodbye, Mrs. Selby it was nice to meet you," I call after her. The minute she leaves, Martin bursts into tears. What I thought was a tough cookie is transformed into a soft marshmallow. Poor Martin!

"Martin, why don't we go inside the room?"

"You've done it now. I'll probably have to stay here all day." Martin sniffs louder. "You know something," he says to me as I hand him a tissue, "my mother doesn't like you. My father doesn't like you. And when I tell my brother what you did, he will kill you."

Martin blows his nose and walks into the room.

Do I get to choose the form my foreshadowed death will take? No airplane or automobile crashes. They're too violent and noisy. Anything a little less dramatic and relatively fast or pain-free will suit just fine.

"Well, I'm glad you're here anyway. It's against the law to stay out of school at your age." Just what is his age? I search my memory banks for the birth date listed in his file but draw a blank. "How old are you, Martin?"

"Eight years old." he says with all the nonchalance of a cavalier man of thirty. "Well, I'm not afraid of those cops. I'll just get in my space mobile and take off for Mars. You'll see."

Either Martin has a well-seasoned sense of humor or his sense of reality isn't quite intact. Flip a coin—heads he does, tails he doesn't.

"Where's your space mobile, Martin?"

"Where all the other space mobiles are; that's a dumb question." Can my ego withstand all this deflation?

"Where are all the other space mobiles?"

"They're lost in space but I will rescue them."

Martin swings an imaginary sword in the air, making his own sound effects: blades swishing, keystone cops dying off in rapid succession. By his form, you would believe he has studied martial arts for at least a decade. When the reality of his predicament sinks in, Martin blubbers like a baby with a huge safety pin sticking to his skin rather than to his diaper.

"Where did you ever learn to fence like that?" I inquire casually and ignore the tears dribbling down his face like rain down a windshield.

"From the television. You can learn a lot from the television." Martin blows his nose and it squeaks.

"Well, Martin, since you're the first one in the room, where do you think you'd like to sit? Where would you be able to do your best work and be on your best behavior?"

He struts around the room, gravely studying the floor plan and the question.

"H'mm-mm, let me think now." Martin tests out each seat, checks the contents of all the desks, and strokes an imaginary beard.

"This is going to be a most interesting year," I muse while Martin investigates.

Finally, he chooses one of the desks near teacher. His baby face creeps through after all. For all his seeming posturing of manliness and noble Englishman affectations, Martin's insides are made of American bubble gum.

"That's a wise choice. May I ask why you picked that desk?"

"Yes, you may." He coughs, clearing his throat and straightens a tie that isn't there as he delivers his public address. "I chose this for the simple reason that when I raise my hand you will see it. See."

"Yes, I do." The door opens and a woman in her mid-fifties hobbles in. I see the flickering of a pink sweater behind her, but like rabbit's ears it appears and disappears.

"Are you Beverly's teacher?" says a short, salt and pepper gray-haired woman with a large voice and a thick body concealed by a loose fitting beige cotton dress that is not only outdated but most unflattering.

"Beverly Crimp?" I ask. Martin howls at the mention of the name and slaps his desk for emphasis.

"Oh, no," his dark eyes roll. "What a crew this is going to be."

"Yes, are you her teacher?"

"Yes, I'm Miss Randolph. It's so nice to meet you."

"Yes, it's good to finally meet you too. I'm Eleanor Crimp." Mrs. Crimp powerfully shakes my hand.

"Where's Beverly?" I ask curiously.

"Anyone can see she's hiding behind that woman. Anyone who's not blind can see that," Martin proclaims, glaring at me with boredom and impatience. His presence isn't to be overlooked; he'll make sure of that.

I look behind Mrs. Crimp and there is a little girl in chestnut brown pigtails cowering against her mother.

"You must be Beverly."

Two brown saucers look up at me, and I behold a smooth face. The pink wool of her sweater is in her mouth. She bends her head again and doesn't answer.

"Are you dumb, girl?" Martin has become the commentator, roving reporter and director.

"Martin!" I interject. That's not a kind way to talk to Beverly. She's just arrived in our class, like you, and we're all going to talk to each other nicely. That's how it works here."

"Humph."

"No," Beverly says shyly to the floor, answering her interlocutor as if I were not there and had never spoken. "I not dun."

"Beverly, I have to get back now. Give Mommy a kiss and be a big girl for the teacher."

Beverly leans into her mother and buries her head in her mother's skirt. When her mother departs, Beverly has no one to hide behind. In the middle of the floor she stands, one foot on top of the other as if to hold herself in place. The sweater hasn't come out of her mouth. I look at the buttons around the collar and notice that the edges are jagged where they've been gnawed. Gypsy moths and English noblemen—the population of my class is certainly becoming diversified. What next?

"Thought you might be looking for this one," the gym teacher says impatiently. "She was wandering all over the first floor."

"Thanks, I appreciate your help." My words soften his face into a weak smile.

"Eva," I grin with every part of me, "Eva, welcome back. I've missed you."

Eva sees me, smiles and quickly turns away. Her hands jut out in front of her, flapping wildly. Not too fast. I've been sitting on my eagerness for days now. I fight back an impulse to rush towards her and grab her up in my arms.

"Well, it appears you two already met." Martin can't stand to be on the sidelines for a second.

"Yes, Martin. Eva was in this class last year. Eva, Martin and Beverly are you ready? Let's find each of you a special seat and a desk of your very own. Martin's already picked out his seat. Beverly, you're next. Where would you like to sit?"

"I don' nooo."

"Well, as long as it's nowhere near me," says Martin. "How old are you, Beverly?" He addresses his audience directly.

"I don' nooo."

Eva moves towards Martin and sniffs him. For some reason, he makes more allowance for this than he does for Beverly's ambiguity.

"Eva, if you want to, you may sit near me." A magnanimous gesture uttered by Martin.

"Eva, where do you want to sit?" I ask.

"—Want to sit?"

"Want to sit, want to sit," Martin mimics, not in malice but in jest. Eva giggles at Martin's imitation and goes over to him and gets a second whiff. Martin sniffs Eva back. Eva glides to where Beverly stands and sniffs Beverly.

"Stinks," Eva says as she runs sideways, flapping her arms again.

There's no denying that emanating from Beverly is a smell not akin to roses. It's a smell of stale urine that's been absorbed in her clothes. Martin finds Eva's honesty nothing less than delightful.

"Beverly stinks, Beverly stinks. I knew there was something wrong with that girl. She stinks. Don't sit near me. Better sit in the back, Beverly, so no one can smell you."

Martin enjoys his own humor and guffaws with exaggerated loudness. Eva flops down in a chair near Martin, and Martin protectively pushes his desk a little closer to Eva's.

"Eva, is that going to be your seat?"

"— Seat," Eva repeats, dazed by all the activity.

"Can't you see she has chosen to sit near to me and not that silly bumpkin?"

I choose Beverly a seat. Otherwise we'd be there forever. Beverly is agreeable. This way she doesn't have to make any choices; it's all done for her. On with it, please, let's get further than the seating arrangements.

"Am I going to be the only boy in this class?" Martin asks.

"No, Ricardo is supposed to come this week and there will be other boys, too."

"Whew, that's more like it."

I make some rules to create order and a sense of routine for them. No hurting one another: respect for each other's bodies, property and personal space. Work must be completed to the best possible standard we can manage. Game time is after all work gets done.

Eva tunes out and hums to herself with talking fingers. Martin's tears surface again, more quietly. They spill onto his desk. Let them go by unnoticed; let him have his dignity. If Martin fights to keep the tears quiet, I won't call attention to them.

Eva can't stay in her seat for too long; she's on the rug, back into the dream state I remember so well.

Kaye enters the room.

"Who's that?" Martin is distrustful of a new person. How quickly territory is established.

"This is Miss Kaye. Good Morning, Miss Kaye," I smile. "And this is Martin, Beverly, and on the rug over there is Eva."

"Hello children," Kaye grins, trying not to stare at Eva.

Eva peeks through the spaces between her fingers and continues rocking. Name tags made by Kaye are put across everyone's desk. Martin cleans his fingernails and searches for moons under his cuticles. The only way I know Beverly's alive under her pink sweater is by her moving mouth as she eats her way through the fabric. Miraculously we make it to lunchtime.

"Man, am I hungry," Martin volunteers.

"How's your stomach pain, Martin?" I tease playfully.

He ignores me and carefully opens his bologna sandwich. Martin's manners are impeccable. Eva still uses her fingers half the time, while Beverly eats her sandwich on the side of the mouth that her sweater isn't on.

Kaye is real quiet, observing and sizing everything up. Her silent question is like my own and everyone else's: Can we live here together in this space for the next ten months? Time will be our fortune teller. Let's hope she is kind!

September 11

Into the room walks a slim, attractive smiling woman, with dark wavy hair down to her shoulders and a boy with hair which conceals most of his hazel eyes. Ricardo. Introductions are made.

"I hope this works out," Mrs. Luciano confides. "The last school he was at couldn't control him. They kicked him out."

"Don't worry, Mrs. Luciano, I'm sure this time will be different." When I look at Ricardo, I see a little boy wearing a scowl. Not just his face, his entire body and stance are one frowning, scowling mass of scrawny flesh. As Mother prepares to leave, she kisses Ricardo on the cheek. A kiss he pretends not to acknowledge.

"Bye, Ma," he says softly as an afterthought when his mother is well out the door and out of hearing range. She probably didn't even hear him.

We find Ricardo a seat. Manner and gesture are docile. So what did he get kicked out of school for, I wonder. I remember reading his file which mentioned the frequent outbursts and class disturbances. Nothing that I believe justified kicking him out of school. I decide to do some more research to learn as much as I can about him and the incident that forced him out of school.

Eva sniffs Ricardo and he uncomfortably brushes his face to eradicate all traces of her.

"Aw, whad'ya do that for?"

"She likes to smell people," Martin, our interpreter, pipes up. Ricardo sits down in an unhappy, uncomfortable slouch and stays like that for most of the day.

I begin to test for math and reading levels. Only Martin is outwardly unruffled by the procedure. Beverly chews on today's frayed yellow sweater and answers every question of mine with a small, "I don' 'oo."

Ricardo sits stolid and mute. I decide we'll give him a little more time.

Lunch is the only activity which enlivens the crew. In eating, they display a passion evident at no other time throughout the day.

Under Beverly's seat is a puddle.

"Beverly, do you want to come to the bathroom with me?" I ask softly.

"No."

"Are you sure? Come on, come with me and we'll get you cleaned up."

For a split second Beverly's eyes turn to me as if to say, 'Are you crazy?' She acquiesces, but refuses to take my hand as we walk to the bathroom.

The children are all shrouded in their separate lives as they watch each other with misgiving and caution. Will someone please tell a joke and make us laugh?

September 16

Eva's bus is early today so Eva is the first inside the classroom. When she enters the room and sees me, she smiles. Reaching inside her desk, Eva takes out a catalog I've given her to look at. She studies the catalog in concentrated stockbroker fashion. She reads the words and touches the pictures of all the items she'll order once her stocks are up. Toys! A world of toys has opened up. Eva can now choose what she wants. The ability to make choices is something she gives to herself. It's a powerful weapon. Not all the sidestepping she does in the room is without purpose; some of it has direction. Eva walks to the game shelf and picks what she wants to play with at game time. Still looking into the catalog of desires, Eva acknowledges my nearness.

"Whose desk is this?" she taps her own desk, waiting for me.

"Eva's desk."

"Whose desk is this?" Her arm stretches, pointing in the direction of my desk.

"Miss Tina's," I answer.

"Whose friend is this?" Eva points to me.

"Miss Tina is Eva's friend."

"And whose friend is this?" Eva points to herself.

"Miss Tina's friend."

For a moment the catalog is forgotten in laughter and real honest-to-goodness, split-second eye contact! I'm beaming that Eva initiated a conversation with me. She quickly shifts her gaze to build her house of toys and games and searches the catalog for pictures. Haven't you heard? A house is to be constructed next to the fortress. One that's Eva's creation: her own blueprint, her own design. Once the house is completed, maybe the rest of the fortress will come down. There are no promises though; we live in the moment here.

Academically, we are at the bottom rung. For all his verbal acrobatics, Martin can read only a few primer words. Beverly auditions to play the shy, retiring child and performs her role admirably: flowers and an Emmy for Bev. What does she really know? What is she thinking when she looks at me with those big oval-shaped browns of hers and won't answer, won't talk? "I don' 'oo" is still her principal mantra. Her statement to the world is a little puddle under her seat. I see the sweaters, of which there are three: pink, yellow and salmon colored — all eaten away, gnawed around the collar and cuffs. Through them she sucks in life in safely cotton-filtered amounts—just a little at a time, too much will intoxicate.

Ricardo bungles everything. His hands always look like he's been working under a car. There are no fingernails. When he was born he chewed them all off. I'm not sure if they've ever returned. The chewing continues; a residual memory of better times. I believe he'd like nothing more than to crawl back into the womb, back to a safe place, a place where he doesn't have to act or resent, a place where he is neither big nor small—the safest place, where he simply is. Ricardo's eyes are always red and puffy; he never stops rubbing them. He's crushed under the slightest refusal or demand. The letter paper he's given every morning is returned to me with raggedy edges, charcoal fingerprints, and is torn and crumpled from the numerous times it's been thrown on the floor. Not to mention the breakfast stains of sticky buns, grape jelly and corn muffins with blotches of chocolate milk. Ricardo's labor is one hour of agonizing drudgery mingled with anger, sweat and tears. And he despises me for making him do it.

Eva reads on a beginning second grade level. We've given her a reading book and a notebook to write down all the new words to remember. Eva's handwritten words, thick and round like caterpillars, swarm the page. Words have come alive for her. Eva also reads with Kaye at Kaye's desk. We are coming together.

Martin hates math; it eludes him. He's majoring in daydreaming and his council of imaginary companions that sometimes give him advice, instruction, and grief when he doesn't conform to their will. Does he really believe they exist? He and Ricardo fry each other with their verbal insults, stalking from a safe distance, looking for the traps each one plants for the other.

And Patty? There is no Patty. She's been written off this planet, shot out of a cannon into space. No trail, no entrails, nothing is left of her. The family moves at every full moon. Mother's fingers are painted pale yellow, moon glow and all the children live on cream cheese. That's all—just cream cheese. No bagels, no hot milk. The courts are attempting to tailgate the family now, checking all agencies for missing persons, looking for the cheese witch and her brood. Missing persons are everywhere. How do you find a family gone AWOL? When they're ready to come out of hiding, they'll appear.

Martin brought his fears to school this week. He carries them in his pocket, some he cradles in his arms. Not all his fears, he's saved the deep ones. Those he can't expose to the sunlight or to himself, yet. At seven and a-half years old, Martin sits on his childhood as if it were an overstuffed trunk. When he tries to seal it up tight, the top opens and a shirt sleeve hangs down. If he plays the flamboyant blaze of psychosis, maybe we'll let him keep his invisible companions in the name of insanity. Heaven forbid it's because he's a little boy. Squash that. Sit on it. Shhhh. He doesn't find the verbal lobotomies he performs on Ricardo alarming or unfair, but he's afraid of the retaliation. His toy soldier veneer peels away once Ricardo leans in with his balled up fists.

"Cut it out!" Ricardo's voice sizzles.

After lunch, the sky darkens suddenly and the class feels heavy and layered in gloom. Everyone falls silent in the wake of the imminent rainstorm.

Martin looks out the window; the stern face is replaced by a sallow frightened one. The evenness and overly assured bellow of his voice has a small rattle in it.

"Are we staying here all night?"

"No, Martin, the sky is dark like that because it's going to rain."

"I can't stay here, I must go home." Martin quavers, little boy sobs heave up and down in his chest.

"It's all right, Martin, you will go home the same time you always do. It's just dark because it's going to rain."

"It's not night?"

"No, it's not night."

"Oh."

"Would you like to finish your math paper at my desk?"

Martin takes all day to complete his math work. He tells me that if he could, he'd let his friend Mister X do it but mathematics is not one of his friend's strong points. His mother already clued me in about Mister X so I'm glad he's bringing this imaginary character out in the open, here. Maybe the other characters will also be revealed in time.

Martin doesn't answer my question, but comes up to my desk in response to the invitation. From his new seat he watches the sky, scans it like a searchlight beam, and waits for a signal. The rain drips slowly down the windows and thunder explodes in the sky. Martin slides his chair a little closer to me. In expectation of the roof caving in on his head, he ducks. There's no place to hide.

"What time is it?" he questions.

"It's time to get your math done so you can have playtime." I advise.

"My mother wants me home. My mother needs me."

That's a switch, an interesting projection of his feelings.

"Martin, I promise you with all my heart when your bus gets here, you will go home."

Martin cries and talks to Mister X out of the side of his mouth, Bogart fashion.

"Don't worry; I won't let her keep you here all night. I'm planning our escape right now," he whispers to his imaginary companion.

When Martin's bus finally arrives, he waves goodbye to our sinking ship from the pier. With raised voice and lunchbox, he calls out in a last moment of gaiety.

"Miss Tina, you're a good woman." And he's off, his white ascot blowing breezily on the wings of his freedom.

"Thanks, Martin." His words will bolster me in the days to follow.

September 22

"Beverly, do you know when you have to go to the bathroom? Do you feel something in your tummy, down here?" I touch her bladder.

"No-ooo." The sound is a soft purr from a mouth which doesn't move. The words steal from the yellow sweater she sucks on.

"There's something like a bag in everyone's tummy, called a bladder, down here." I point to my own bladder. "When it's time to go to the bathroom or to pee, the bag or bladder fills up with urine or pee and we feel full. That's how we know when we need to go to the bathroom, because it feels funny in our bladders. Do you feel anything before you have to go to the bathroom?"

"Nooooo."

"That's okay, Bev. Maybe next time you can watch for those feelings in your bladder. If you feel them first, they will help you know when to go to the bathroom so you can make it on time. Okay?"

*A little girl wrapped in her mother's dresses,
her mother's fading vision. Beverly walks inside the footsteps of her mother's slow hesitant
gait. She is weary, living like a shadow within
her mother's life so that she can't feel her own.
How can she feel her urine dripping down her
legs? They are not her legs. She has borrowed
those thick legs from underneath her mother's
skirts and she pulls them along with her like dead
weights, dragging them along as the cross she
bears through life.*

*She has hidden under the old wrinkled hands of
her mother, listening to tales of devils and demons
emptying the fear and terror into a muddy puddle
underneath her feet.*

I wonder if she does feel the urine as it trickles steamy and wet down her leg. Maybe the only sensation Beverly feels in the whole world is her urine on its way down her leg onto the floor.

Eva comes in and writes "catalog" on the board, not asking anyone to spell for her. She draws a picture and wants a ribbon to wrap around it like a scroll.

"Who's the picture for, Eva?"

"For Mommy."

"What did you make?"

"Garden. Eva's garden. Eva has a garden."

"It's a lovely garden, Eva," I say as she holds the picture out for me to see. She swirls a green satin ribbon around the drawing and holds onto it all day.

"Ricky, Ricky Ricardo," Martin rumbas near the closet as he hangs up his raincoat.

Ricardo lunges and testily shakes his knuckles in Martin's nose. Martin yelps and inches nearer to adult backup forces. When the coast is clear, he pounds on imaginary bongos and his head and neck gyrate to the rhythms only he is privy to. His hips swivel; his belt is slung low on one thigh.

Music and bravado. What a flair for melodrama and theatrics. If Martin were on stage, portraying a different character every third day, would all his personalities be appeased? This little boy needs a theatre, a home for all his characters and playmates, somewhere they could all live and have life and breath, and costumes and audiences.

"I'm not going to do that goddamned paper. Don't give a shit. I'm not gonna do a damned thing in here," Ricardo hisses.

Ricardo, our little lion cub has awakened. He unfurls his fangs from his twin heads and throws a fang at me. It misses. The poison threads its way down the aisle of the room.

"If you don't do the paper, there will be no play. Work comes first. I know it's hard. It can't always be easy. I know it takes time to get it right. It's okay. What you do will be fine. You just have to try Ricardo, that's all."

"You're a damned pain in the butt, you know that?"

A slew of profanities cannot remove my presence or the discomfort of my words. The jelly spaces of his being I see into like a seer. I've kept my expectations of him minimal, to give him the space to find some ease in himself. We can focus on academic targets when some of the social elements are more comfortable for him. When he works it's almost painful to watch. He struggles as if there are two armed men at his back, jabbing their pistols in his ribs. He knows he's clumsy; he can't focus or concentrate. He has those guns in his flesh and it's a matter of living and dying. School is reduced to sheer survival; the armed men are relentless. They're never satisfied with what he produces and everything seems to come about forcibly. Forget about doing well in school. There is no amount of joy. It's only about surviving, not only the task, but the whole unpleasant ordeal of school and living. And what's worse is that Ricardo believes that he's doomed. Doomed to fail and doomed to punishment, a life that's difficult with relentless hit men always pointing out his failures and inadequacies to him. He has three papers to complete.

A task that can easily be accomplished with little effort, Ricardo refuses to tackle. He acknowledges failure before he's begun, never to experience the satisfaction of completion.

Ricardo kicks the paper around the floor. He throws his chair across the room away from the other children. It lands in the play area.

> *He was born on Mount Olympus where the rest of the gods live and he has swallowed ten dragons whole that live inside him where it gets smoky and hot. They make him irritable, they give him colic and he wishes he'd never swallowed them. He regrets his existence.*
>
> *Burdensome it is, ten dragons eating his stomach from the inside out and he must keep up appearances too. After all, someday he'll be a big man, a proud man like his father.*
>
> *Mothers are for bullying. No matter how much that feeling inside of your gut says hug your momma, let her hold you, ignore it. It's the voice of weakness sidling along next to you, the voice of trouble.*
>
> *Women are for leering at and coming home to late at night when they're already in bed and you can grab them furtively and hard, fingering the darkness, thumping the sheets with your body.*
>
> *And little boys, they're little gods, and they must never forget that, not for a moment.*

Ricardo wants to play more than he wants to be a god. He kicks the desk legs as he works, but finishes his paper, muttering and cursing me under his breath.

"Ricardo, I'm so proud of you. You did it!"

"Yeah, whatever; who cares, anyhow?"

"I care," I smile into his furtive eyes.

Team Tactics

September 28

Kaye's desk and mine are pulled together. Sometimes we need to sit back: two conspirators who watch the war rather than participate. It feels like war when the classroom becomes a battleground of wills and lobbying for the upper hand. With so many daily battles and skirmishes, sometimes Kaye and I stand back to see how the children are faring in their attempts at freedom, tyranny, and socializing. At the end of the day, we're all on the same side. The only way to win the war, and win the war we will, is to unite everyone. Sometimes they fight us; sometimes they battle each other and more often they're at odds with themselves. Someday they'll understand that this place, this classroom is their sanctum and all of us, including Kaye and me are their allies. All in good time, I believe.

Beverly works on identifying colors and shapes. She won't look at them. The 'I don' oo' comes before the question's even asked. She watches the others longingly as they play with the trucks and toys in the sandbox. She won't go back there to the play area. Possibly the best thing that will ever happen to Bev in her whole life waits in that place with rugs on the floor and a kitchen with a stove and a sink. Dolls. Right there, just several meters away, dead center in her line of vision, and she doesn't know it. Watch it slide right by her without any objection. She'll never miss it. She didn't know what it was about from the beginning. So why worry about it? Why lose sleep over it? She doesn't.

*Her nightmares are of the devil coming to her
in a dark, stale smelling house. She's lying in bed
without enough pillows to smother the fear that's
crushing her. Cold fingers of fear choke the air out
of her. She is quiet, she is not breathing, and the
devil enters her room.*

*In the morning she remembers he came into her
bedroom because she did something bad. What was
it? What had she done? That's it, she remembers as
she chews on her pink sweater. She ate the last of
the cookies in the box.*

*Yeah, the devil took care of her 'cause she was
bad and ate the cookies. And her momma said she
was bad. And now she knows.*

We come together as a group for our morning language arts story.
The only bright-eyed creature of the morning is Martin who delights
in finding fault with the entire planet. If he were in control (and he's
working on it, as soon as he learns to compute two plus four), Martin
would run the entire operation like a circus. He would be master of
ceremonies, the ticket taker, the producer, and occasionally double
for the lion. But he's not in control. Someone else is. That someone
else is always telling him what to do. Just like he tells the others, it
tells him, "Now, Martin..." the voice says.

"Does anyone have any news?" I ask with a burst of energy.

"Nah," Ricardo slumps down in his chair and kicks the floor
with his holey sneaker.

"I do, I do," Martin's hand mows the air at 35 m.p.h.

"Okay, Martin, what news would you like to tell us about?"

"Well, you see, today Curly, now he's the man who lives on
Dewey Street, one block down from Cherry, where I live, only he
lives at 704, and I live at 646 but it doesn't matter." A pause, as he
gazes out tenderly into his audience.

"Now, where was I?" His hand, palm upward rises to his head, chin upturns, a little profile. Ah, he almost has it. Now where was he in the script? "You see, Curly gulps down his coffee fast 'cause he has somewhere to go and he's in a hurry."

"Whoa, Martin," I call out. "You want me to write all this on the board? I'll never be able to fit everything. What happened to Curly?"

"Curly smashed up his car. He went around the turn and didn't see the other car coming and C-R-U-N-C-H head on. Curly didn't know what hit him. He smashed in his whole front end. What a shame. Poor Curly."

"Was everyone all right?"

"Yeah, nobody was hurt, just the cars. And now they're ready for Mission Trash Can." At this point the trumpets blow and Martin flies off like Super Man, only he's masked.

"Aw, that didn't happen, he made the damned thing up. He's a liar, what a liar."

"Ricardo, do you have any news for us?"

"Yeah, my father drove me to school today in his Cadillac."

"Your father doesn't have a Cadillac, Ricardo. He has a blue 1969 Ford," utters none other than the whiz kid, and spoken like a state trooper.

"Oh yeah, turkey, how d'ya know what my father has? Think you're smart, smart nothin'. You don't know nothin', you little punk dummy."

"I saw your car when your father drove you to school. It was last Wednesday. And the car was blue."

"That was my brother's car. Stupid. What, don't ya think my brother's got a car too? We all got cars. I got one just waitin' for me for when I'm eighteen. Ya damn punk."

On the board, "Ricardo's father drove him to school in his Cadillac."

Do I believe it? No, of course not, but I must keep up pretenses myself. The truth is not good enough for Ricardo. He has to gloss up the truth with glitter and Gargantua. Only then can he present himself. I have to respect this, I don't want him to feel too vulnerable and exposed.

"Miss Tina, he doesn't have a Cadillac, really."

Ricardo lunges and smashes Martin's chin with a hard right.

"Cut it out, Ricardo," cries Martin as he inches away, collecting his troops and his hat for the retreat.

"Ow, stop, sto—o-o—p!"

"Okay, Ricardo, no fighting. Remember the rules."

"Well, he better cut it out, he better keep to his own stupid self and mind his own business or I'm gonna kill that faggot."

Ricardo recovers his composure and the cosmetic face the class wears is back on.

"Beverly, do you have any news for us?"

"Nooo." Bev looks down.

"No news at all?" I ask encouragingly.

"Nooo."

"No, No, No," Martin's regained his sense of humor and falsetto voice. He mimics Beverly in operetta style.

Ricardo grins despite the malice he has for Martin. The comic wins out. Once again, Martin has his audience where he wants them.

"Eva, do you have any news?"

"Friday is Eva's birthday." Eva stands up awkwardly.

"It is not, she made it up."

"It is her birthday. Eva is right. October 3 is Eva's birthday."

Martin salutes Eva and hums "Happy Birthday." I write it down and Kaye and I look at each other. We have to make plans. Thanks to Eva and Martin, details like birthdays are not forgotten here.

Our morning story is completed. Eva reads it. Martin recites it from aural memory and Ricardo stumbles through it, repeating the words after I've said them for him. Beverly won't try.

October 3

Today is Eva's birthday. I am as excited as if it were my own. Another year in which Eva has embraced so much of life one can't count it like the number of candles on a birthday cake.

Martin's chubby face and smoothed down hair appear at the door first. He enters humming "Happy Birthday" and "For She's a Jolly Good Fellow" and replays his rendition from 9 AM till countdown. Dutifully, he brings Eva a card from his home. Martin is all pomp and ceremony. You would think the card came from the palace of the king; and he's the noble messenger, replete with royal horn and costume. 'Sir Martin' rides to school without his horse. It's a good thing, too. If he brought the horse, he would tire out the animal. Martin exists solely on electrical energy. He is input and output, receiver and transmitter, the whole shebang. Starring Martin Selby, featuring Martin Selby, and presenting none other than Martin Selby. He's a world unto himself. But what's that he's picking up on his antennae? It seems like other worlds are always attempting to contact him. Martin stands ever ready to decode and serve. He has sworn his allegiance and, true to his words, his armor and shield stand ready for defense. But it's his mouth which is always on the offensive. His mouth has been responsible for many wars, casualties, and defection by at least two-thirds of his own army. Still he goes on, smiling through his tears, his mishaps and his near-demise.

"Good morning, Miss Tina, Miss Kaye. Where's the birthday girl?"

"She hasn't come in yet, Martin. How are you today?"

"Just fine, Miss Kaye. I'm waiting for the birthday girl. I have an important message to deliver to her."

"Do you think it can wait till she gets here?" I ask.

"Yes, I suppose so, but it can't wait forever. It must be done to-day or else—" Martin decapitates himself with his fingers.

Followed by Martin's dramatics is Ricardo, who pushes open the classroom door as if it were a swinging saloon door and he's just returning from a street brawl.

"Hello, Ricardo, Hello, Ric-car-do. Hel-lo, Ri-car-do," and other variations of the motif boom from our resident actor, Martin, ad-libbing every line.

"Hi." Real small, like it would fit down a mouse hole. That's how small.

And then to Martin, "Look, you son of a hua. Shut your mouth today 'cause I ain't in a good mood, see, and I'll get ya."

Martin smiles. He has created friction and an electric jolt in his arm tells him it's wonderful. He's all charged up and ready for some more. The red flashing alarm signal in his brain is activated by the general who has just given orders to kill on sight anything that moves.

The only moving object is Ricardo, as he hangs his light cotton denim jacket in the closet.

"I've got a secret. I've got a secret. And Ricardo doesn't know the secret. Ricardo doesn't know. It's Martin's secret. And Eva's secret. And Ricardo doesn't know. No, Ricardo doesn't know."

Martin's kicked in the rear; cries of woe and real tears surface.

"Miss Tina! Help! Help! Now, stop it, Ricardo!"

"Okay, let's stop fighting, boys. Maybe if you didn't tease Ricardo, he wouldn't hurt you. He doesn't like to be teased."

"Neither do I, and that is no lie."

Beverly peeks in.

"Hi," she says shyly and tiptoes to her seat.

> *If only the floor would rise up and conceal her entrance, then she wouldn't feel embarrassed. If she would just become invisible overnight, she wouldn't feel her bones all protrusive and awkwardly extended. Angular, at right angles to herself and never making contact. There's a point at her chin, one at her head, two angles at her elbows, two more on her knees. She is all angles, and points on angles, and she doesn't see any point to herself. She is full of angles and demons and no answers.*
>
> *The world's not a disappointment, it's a mistake. No, she's the mistake. And she lives in a house with cobwebs and bats. She lives within the fears of her*

*mother's twisted dresses and hangs with them silent
and drab in the closet.*

"Well, well, if it isn't, uh, Miss Beverly herself." Martin struts
with his hand on his hip. "And how do you smell this morning?"

He and Ricardo roll on the floor in hysterics. Ricardo loves when
Martin's acumen is pointed in another's direction. Anyone else can
be the butt of Martin's biting wit, as long as it's not him.

"Yeah, Beverly, how's your smelly self this morning?" Ricardo
chimes in.

"Listen, boys, I thought we talked about not teasing each other.
Both of you said you didn't want to be teased. Now you're teasing
Beverly when you don't like it done to you."

"But you see, Miss Tina," Martin's holding his insides so the
spasms of laughter don't spill out, "she's different."

"She has feelings just like you and Ricardo do."

"Yeah, but," Martin giggles on his words, "she stinks." His eyes
roll one hundred eighty degrees. Martin somersaults.

Ricardo laughs till the dirt and tears are streaking down his face.

"Put it there, Martin," Ricardo holds out his hand. "Slip me five,
Ricardo my man."

*They walk up to the bar and Ricardo buys the
first round. They laugh into the suds of camaraderie
and clap each other on the back in manlike fashion.
They've become men at the expense of another. Their
friendship is too dear to relinquish; they know it comes
and goes.*

*Each of them keeps one hand on the side of the
holster where the gun rests—just in case. A beer's a
beer but, just in case, the gun is loaded.*

*Martin's never shot a gun in his whole life, but
it's loaded. He believes he can outtalk anybody and
maybe he's right. Ricardo's afraid he'll use the gun*

*too soon, and fire all his bullets, then find out he
enjoys it and run around shooting like the guys he
hears about on television: the ones who shoot from
the rooftops: All innocent victims dead.*

*One day he might just blow everybody to bits,
till their red wet insides go flying all over the place.
And he won't stop even then, he's afraid there won't
be anyone to stop him. They'll all be dead. His hand
trembles against the gun in the holster.*

"Aw, Beverly," Martin winks at Ricardo. "We're real sorry. We didn't mean to call you stinky."

Again they laugh as Martin twists the knife just one more turn. He's bargaining for Ricardo's friendship, and he wants it real bad.

"Yeah, re-eeal sorry," his buddy assents.

Beverly watches them. Somewhere inside her she knows she's been jabbed but she's not sure where. It hurts everywhere. One more wound, one more scar. She's never known anything different. It's not so bad because at least it's real familiar. No surprises. Beverly sits down and watches the two boys arm wrestle.

"Boys, now it's work time. Save the wrestling match for later. Remember the rules. Work has to be finished. No fighting and no teasing. You are very close to losing playtime this afternoon."

"You really know how to spoil a good thing."

Nevertheless, Martin takes his seat. If he didn't, his guilt-ridden conscience would keep him up all night without promises of oatmeal cookies and warm apple cider. Just belittlement and you should have's. His wit is powerless against his conscience, which is a strange conglomerate of his mother's voice, his father's moustache, and his brother's newly acquired beard. It has his aunt Jean's clacking tongue, and Uncle Max's cigars and his cousin Edna's in there too. They're all dressed in Martin's clothes and Martin's body and make living inside him real uncomfortable at times. It's insulting how they carry on. But there are other forces. Martin's outer-terrestrial companions will smite the others, only they haven't been able to yet. He's working on it.

In walks Eva.

"Today is my birthday. I am eight years old. Today is my birthday, October 3."

"Eva, just the one I want to see. I have a message for you. You must read it. Your life depends upon it. Here." Martin fumbles in his pocket and produces an immaculate envelope with Eva's name on it.

Eva grins and sniffs it.

"Open it, open it."

Eva's fingers cannot open it, and Martin assists.

"A card, Martin gives Eva a card," Eva comments as she examines and sniffs and holds the card up to her eyes.

"Read it," Martin commands.

Eva reads slowly. Her voice lacks cadence.

"Martin, that's really kind of you to get Eva a card. Eva, aren't you going to thank Martin?" Kaye walks closer to the duo.

"Thank you," Eva gallops sideways to the back of the room, holding the card out like a wand and shaking it excitedly inside her clasped fingers.

"Aw, it's a lousy card, I bet you found it on the way to school 'cause you're so cheap." Ricardo sulks.

"I did not. My mother and I bought it together and I picked it out."

"You picked it out? You can't even read!"

"My mother read it to me. And I can read better than some people I know with the initials R. L."

Ricardo chases Martin around the room and tackles him.

"Ow! Now, Ricardo, you stop it! Miss Kaye! Miss Tina!"

"Okay, you have ten seconds to get in your seats. It's time for our news. We have many activities to finish today and a special surprise." Surprise? Ricardo stiffens with Martin's legs in his grip.

I am Santa Claus. I am the witch queen. I am the nice lady around the corner who always gives candy and raisins to the kids.

A promulgation of 'surprise' and elves walked in carrying candy canes and gobs of chocolate ice cream. Daubing little girls' toenails candy apple red, they stuff little boys' mouths with bazooka gum while slapping baseball cards into their open palms. Ricardo releases Martin's legs to the floor and walks back to his seat. Martin sits and brushes the dust off his pants.

"Surprise, surprise," Eva dances back to us, sits on the edge of her chair about to spring up again at any moment.

We have Eva's party in the afternoon. Kaye takes Eva outside for a walk in the hall while the rest of us put candles on the cake. Nine candles, one is for good luck. We are superstitious and we believe in rituals.

Martin and Ricardo fight about who's going to turn off the lights.

"I'm going to let Beverly do it," I say firmly.

"That toad, she can't do anything."

"Yeah, she can't do anything."

Still in Ricardo's camp, Martin finds a way to get into the act.

"Come on, Beverly, I'll help you. It's real easy."

Martin offers his hand, which has flecks of courage at the fingertips. Beverly walks up to the light switch; her life and her status in the group are connected with this one deed. She closes her eyes and the lights go out. Martin and I cheer.

"Aw, she's just a dumb girl," Ricardo maligns.

Beverly is ecstatic. She grins with every muscle in her face. An act of heroism, she liked it. She likes it so much she wants to repeat the performance and turn the lights on and off, off and on, just to feel powerful, recreating that one instant when she makes the room dark and light again.

Kaye and Eva walk in and we sing (rather Kaye and I sing while Martin bellows) "Happy Birthday." Eva's fingers flutter in excitement. When the candles are all blown out by Eva and Mister X, we clap.

"Open the present, Eva." I nudge her. Eva opens the wrapping. Inside is a Barbie coloring book and box of crayons.

"Barbie," Eva murmurs, "a Barbie doll book."

Kaye helps Eva cut the cake into slices while Martin smacks his lips.

"Boy, am I gonna love to get my jaws into that."

It's chocolate, it's creamy, gooey, and looks delicious and that's why Ricardo hates it. Ricardo bites into the cake and makes faces like it was laundry detergent rather than moist carbohydrate flakes bursting in his mouth. Just to prove he's not a fledgling in gluttony, he gobbles all the cake and sucks on the chocolate residue from his fingers like a human vacuum cleaner.

Beverly's face has a hundred fifty watt bulb inside of it. She eats slowly, savoring every sugary morsel, assuming it will never come 'round again. With relish and noises of contentment, Martin devours his cake. It's on Eva's nose, outlining her lips like lipstick. She could finger paint her birthday cake, hand paint it all over the walls. It's her birthday, so I refrain from scolding. Kaye's viscera are not as strong as mine. She looks away and then hands Eva a pink napkin.

At playtime, Eva colors in her new book. Beverly sits in her chair gazing at the light switch in befuddled wonderment. Did she really do all that?

Martin has to finish his math. It's too quiet for Ricardo, too settled; he's itchy. He grabs the card Martin has given to Eva and sails it across the room. Eva wails and pulls at her hair.

"Noooo, give it back, give it back." Eva screams. She rips the page she's coloring and then slams the book repeatedly against the desk.

Alarmed by Eva's unearthly display of rage, Ricardo flips the card towards her but not before he makes sure one of the corners is torn.

"Give it to me, give it to me!" Eva screams.

Martin picks the card up and hands it to Eva, who swings at him. Everyone is suddenly quiet. This is one side of Eva they've not encountered before. Seeing it for the first time jolts them into sobriety.

Eva cries and rocks herself in the chair.

"Eva did that. Ricardo did that!" I tape the picture and the card, but it's not the same.

"Ricardo, you've lost the rest of your game time. Sit down, please."

He complies, but only because the room feels like a tomb and the silence is deadly even for him. The day ends on a somber note despite the birthday celebration.

I meet Stella at Bar Koko for a glass of wine after work. Each day's so exhausting; sometimes it's easy to forget about life outside the school. It feels great to laugh and drink and catch up. We put the world to rights over a bottle of Cabernet and mushroom pizza. Sometimes the truth and the lightness of things really lay in comfort food and the familiar warmth and understanding of a dear friend. She made me laugh with tales of her latest beau, Nate. They're most definitely not each other's type, yet are having an amazing time together with nothing in common but their inexplicable desire for each other.

I think she cares about him even more than she admits to herself. Who am I to judge the compatibility of two people? After all, there is that familiar saying about opposites attracting, which seems correct in the case of Stella and Nate. What I also know of Stella is that sometimes she exaggerates to demonstrate the hilarity of the moment. Not to be malicious, never, but to be funny. You can't fault her; she really makes you laugh.

Into the Mix

October 10

Ricardo has declared war. He's expanded the battleground beyond the classroom and to other potential enemies. He's set up bar-
ricades in the halls to ambush other children as they pass by. He
stands at the top of the stairs; he threatens to jump the twenty feet,
clunk to the bottom. The psychological data in his file says he's
extremely violent but they haven't put him behind bars or handed
out tranquilizers to the faculty! Will he injure himself? Is his death
worth that much to him?

He doesn't believe his death is worth as much to us, of that I'm
certain. He scrunches up his face; he greases up his hands before
coming to school and digs out the dirtiest, smelliest shirt he can find
in the laundry basket. He whips up marine green worms from the
ground and cracks them in two at the head, then smears them on his
work papers, stuffs them in his and Bev's desk till days later there is
an unmistakable stench in the room of death and rotting. He wants
us to know what that smell and sense is all about. We might understand about him and how he feels inside.

When I reach out to touch him, he curdles like sour milk. The
date on his container has expired. If he's praised for a gesture, a
button on right, a thin smile, his hands against his ears squelch anything sounding melodious. He'll have nothing to do with it, yet he
can't survive without it any more. The rage in him is rising dan-
gerously and he can't control it any longer. He'd like to nuzzle his
head against a soft furry woolly body for the rest of his lifetime and
never open his eyes. Someone take him and sit with him nestled in

a hammock, in a forest of evergreens, and rock him. Then would the anger abate?

He takes nothing home. The moment he's finished, be it an art project or a math paper, he squeezes the pulp out of it.

> *His pride will be given to him when he turns sixteen, along with a pocket knife, a pack of French playing cards, and the privilege of sitting with the other men.*
>
> *When he was one year old his pride was yanked out of his chest and ceremoniously buried in a grave. A serape was spread over the earth to insulate his pride from cold. As they lowered the box with a piece of him inside, he thought he heard muffled crying.*
>
> *They covered up the wound in the ground with dirt and a prayer; his incision they covered up with a five and dime needle and eighty-five proof alcohol.*
>
> *Sometimes he feels the long crooked line down his chest like a dry brittle ache. Inside the ache is a long corridor left fallow, he feels hollow there, like there's something missing, something that's been prematurely torn from him.*
>
> *When he's sixteen they've promised he can have back his pride. Maybe then the emptiness will go away.*

"Ricardo, it's time to come inside. You can't stand on the stairs all day."

"Come any closer and I'll jump. You hear me! Don't touch me, don't come near me. I'm warnin' ya. I'm gonna jump. I don't care. Just watch me. Stand back."

"It's a long way down. I don't know if you'll be able to climb back up again. Maybe two broken legs, a fractured collar bone,

you'd be in a cast for months. You wouldn't be able to beat up anyone. Probably you wouldn't be able to walk."

Death is easier than the reality of bruises and cracked bones.
Death does you in and it's over, kaput. An injury means you'd
still be here on this earth with more injustices and indignities to
suffer.

Ricardo pretends not to hear me, but he's listening. He backs
slightly away from the banister.

"I'm not gonna come in that room and do all that lousy work and
sit with a bunch of dummies and wisecrackers." At least his conversation has moved away from the landing.

"Well, if you want to stand here all day by yourself without lunch
and play, that's fine. I'm going back in the classroom. When you're
ready you can come back in. Don't let Mr. Donahue catch you out
here without a hall pass. Bye." Bravely I turn, dismissing him, denying him the melodrama in his choice between life and death. The
stage is pulled out from under him. The audience is sent home and
all the lights turned off. He's alone with himself in the darkness
where men and little boys come to terms with that final act. No one
wants to watch the curtain come down for him.

As brave as I appear, I have my doubts but I stick to my decision
and walk back to the classroom. With the grace and lightness of a
cat, Kaye nods to me and slips into the hallway, keeping vigil.

It's pretty monotonous when you're all the way out on the highest tree limb and your stomach is growling and wants to be fed.
After a while there's not much to do but swing your legs and try
to remember why you strayed so far from the others and so near
to lunchtime. The reasons aren't too clear and the mind is dulled.
You're having more fun bashing in other kids and hollering abuses
at the teachers. It gets lonely all the way out there on that limb.
There's a cramp in your leg that longs to be stretched and you gotta
take a piss before your bladder ruptures. So you wait and ease up
slowly like you're thinking real hard and long about this. Weighing
everything, you saunter down the halls like you got all day. Time

is easily on the side of your nine years and you feel cocky because they're all inside working and you're free.

You go to the bathroom and check to see if you're followed, push open the bathroom door with your worn leather boot. Take a leak on the floor and etch out "hua" with your mother's missing fingernail file. Toilet paper is ripped up and thrown around the bathroom like confetti at Mardi Gras. When another boy comes into the bathroom you search his pockets and filch twenty-five cents. To show your gratitude, you poke him in the ribs. He runs off crying and you scream to the bathroom walls, 'son of a hua,' 'son of a hua,' till the cries are lost.

"Okay Ricardo, that's just about enough. If you don't come out of the bathroom, I'm coming in," Kaye's no-nonsense voice intervenes when she sees the other boy race from the bathroom and down the hallway, far away from Ricardo.

Ricardo opens the door and kicks it closed again. He walks back towards the classroom with the silver piece warm and real in his pocket. He doesn't talk to anyone and only Eva acknowledges his homecoming.

"Hi, Ricardo," she sniffs him and runs away to read with Kaye. A wan smile upturns the corners of his face. He fingers the coin and loftily hoists his feet up on the desk.

"Okay, it's almost lunchtime. Martin, you have one more paper to do before you can eat. You don't want to be last again, do you?"

"I can't do it."

"Bring it up here," Miss Kaye suggests. "We'll see what the trouble is. I'm sure you can do it."

Martin beams. He loves praise, armfuls of it. A slow inhalation and I proceed.

"And Ricardo, you have a letter paper to do before lunch. Beverly, would you please pick up the papers on the floor by your desk for me?" I have to bend down and point them out to her, but I won't touch them.

"Les," Bev's voice is hushed.

"I'm not goin' to do any damned papers. I warned you already. I hate this place and everybody in it. And you, you're a witch." Ricardo flings a book at me. Luckily for both of us, his aim is off.

"Miss Tina, look at my math paper. It's all finished. Got it all right, didn't I, Miss Kaye?"

"You sure did, Martin. I knew you could do it." Kaye winks at Martin. Martin's heart flutters.

> *He's in love with an earth woman who is thirty-three years his senior. He'll remove his feathery hat and bow before his grande dame, mistress of octagons and parallelograms, after smoothing his long fine combed moustache. He will gaze amorously into those brown crater eyes of hers and ask her to share his palatial domain and be first mathematician to his kingdom.*
>
> *When she consents, as she must, his mask will disintegrate, his costume dematerialize, and she will behold King Zagoot from Planet Zagoot, in all his ethereal splendor, scintillated, and tinted meteorite green for flash.*

Ricardo hears praise lavished on Martin, his arch rival and best friend. He rips up the paper. T's and H's float on the air like wind-blown cotton candy.

"I can't find my paper."

"That's because it's flying everywhere but in the trash can."

"I don't have my paper."

"Here's another one. Look, I put your name on it. When you're done, put the paper on my desk, please."

"No, I'm not gonna do it."

"Fine. Don't do it. Lunch time is when your work is done."

I hear my firmness like an earth tremor. I hear my mother in her last exasperated moment when nothing will budge me. And followed by a stony silence: a giving up of the dialogue but always with the upper hand.

A chair flies. I'm protected by the invisible shield Martin creates between Ricardo and the rest of us. Sometimes Ricardo's target practice is within bulls-eye range.

>*King Zagoot has contacted Zagoot and is arranging to have Ricardo zagooted there for observation. He admires a specimen of will and courage, plus he loves the accent. King Zagoot will have the court players study it and have them perform in Ricardo's fluid tongue.*
>
>*He will take Ricardo in his space mobile and they will ride on the tails of the shooting stars they chase, he will appoint Ricardo chief of military operations and his planet will be well protected.*
>
>*The Zagootians will love their king and he will reign forever in peacetime.*

"Would you like me to set the table, Miss Tina?" volunteers Martin.

"Yes, that would be very nice. Thank you."

Martin hums as he arranges the place mats and the napkins. This is hand-to-hand combat and Ricardo is losing. No matter how treacherous he appears, the enemy receives the spoils. A book vanishes from his hand and lands on the side of Martin's head.

"Now, Ricardo, stop that. You know you're not supposed to do that. Miss Kayeeee!"

"Ricardo, sit down and do your paper. Leave Martin alone!"

>*The cook surprises King Zagoot with his favorite dessert: coconut cream custard. He is royally happy.*

We sit down to eat. Ricardo scatters papers around the room for attention but we ignore him. My overcooked hot dog tastes like cardboard. I silently remind myself to make time to pack a lunch. Anything is better and more edible than cafeteria style cooking. Life is funny; here I am amid children chomping down on indiscernible animal remnants mashed up and rolled into a long tube-like plastic wrapping, surrounded by fluff that vaguely resembles bread, or is it polystyrene? And the craziest thing? This is my choice. And, crazier still, I just love it. I can't think of anywhere I would rather be right now than sitting here with our crew. I look at Kaye, who winks at me, and I know she feels the same.

> *Not only is there a hole in Ricardo's chest where*
> *they removed his pride but there's a puncture in*
> *his craw craving food to fill it. And there's never*
> *enough food. He is always left stranded and aching*
> *and hungry.*
> *The tide sweeps over him, knocking him down.*
> *Crags perforate his stomach. Anger and food flood*
> *out of him and he is empty, empty, empty.*

"I can't do this damn paper. I don't know how to do this!"

There is a pencil in Ricardo's hand. His mouth is freely negating but his fingers compute the examples.

"Here, I finished your damn paper. Now are ya happy?" The paper lands on the floor.

"Well done, that's great. Put it on my desk, please. Come wash your hands for lunch. And Ricardo, I'm proud of you for doing your work," I say between bites.

"Oh yeah. Well, I ain't doin' any more work in this dinky class."

"Rinky Dinky, Beverly is stinky," Martin chants. The boys laugh. Ricardo sits down next to Martin to join us. His face is a network of creases and pencil smudges, yet magically all his morning work is completed.

October 12

Mr. Strong and I talk in his office after school. He tells me that the principal, Mr. Donahue is getting phone calls from some parents about my class, particularly regarding Ricardo's behavior. He overheard Mr. Donahue speaking with a parent who is concerned about her child's safety.

"Whatever you do Tina, please contain his meltdowns to the classroom or we're going to have some real trouble."

"I know it doesn't look like it from the outside, but Ricardo is making progress," I answer.

"You know I can see that, Tina, but unfortunately many parents are wary about this program and have been from the beginning. And you see how difficult it's been even for some of the teachers to come around. I just don't want all the good that you're doing to be compromised."

"I don't either. Thanks for telling me. If you find out anything else, please share it."

"You know I will," he smiles warmly. "Right now Mr. Donahue is handling everyone, but if that doesn't work, you'll be hearing from him personally."

October 16

Martin plays in the sandbox. I watch as he puts the doll on a sand pile. He takes her pulse and closes the plastic lids of her eyes.

"She's dead," he whispers to himself. "Better cover her up." He crouches down, bending his knees and over the doll's body he spreads white sand, delicately sifting the sand through his fingers.

At the board, Eva prints 'bogey man.'

"There is no bogey man," Eva tells her moving fingers. "Eva and Miss Tina killed bogey man."

The expression on Martin's chubby face has changed from nurturer to disciplinarian. He removes the doll from her burial place and spanks her hard: once, twice, countless times.

"She was bad. She got into some matches. Aren't you ashamed of yourself?" he asks the doll.

"Is I a gel?" Bev asks me.

"Yes, Beverly, you are a girl, a very pretty girl."

"Is you a gel?"

"No, I'm a woman. When you get older you'll be a woman, too."

"Is Eva a gel?"

"Yes, Eva is a girl."

"A gel like me?"

"Yes, a girl just like you."

> *Risking damnation, she tiptoes from under the umbrellas of her mother, searching for her scattered limbs, a mole burrowing in the sloshy mud, she slides and she stumbles, groping for a right hand, a left foot. Can she rescue the fingers? Which way do they fit? Are they upside down? How to make herself whole, she wonders...*
>
> *There is a photograph of a little girl tattooed inside her head. She holds the body parts up to the light to see if they correspond to the image, but she can't tell because she hasn't found her eyes yet. The mud is inching up her dismembered body as she feels herself slowly sinking.*

October 24

It's October. Eva's skipped over this month and the next and parachuted herself right into December and Christmas. She takes stock of all that she wants.

"And I want this and the spelling games and a 'Barbie' doll and a dollhouse and…"

At the blackboard Eva draws a picture of two boots.

"Whose boots are these?" she asks me.

"Eva's boots."

"Eva's got new boots." Eva kicks up her legs for me to admire the boots.

"Eva, the boots are lovely!"

"Mommy bought them for Eva. Eva and mommy, and Eva got new boots."

Eva makes me think of my own mom. I haven't been out shopping with her for years. That used to be something we enjoyed doing together back when I still lived at home. It was a good excuse for some girl time and a good chat. How I miss her.

November 3

"Beverly, how about pulling your chair closer to the desk? I don't want you to fall."

Beverly's sitting with both elbows on the desk and her knees in a sprawl on the leaning chair, which may topple at any moment.

"I fall, I die?"

"No, Bev, I don't think you'll die. I don't want you to get hurt."

"I fall, I be dead?" her eyes scrutinize my face.

"No, you won't be dead."

Beverly has lost the buttons on her yellow sweater. Did she swallow them?

> *One button for a mouth, one button for a nose, two for her eyes. Maybe she can create herself with the ordinary buttons. If she swallows the threads of the sweater, can she sew all the parts of her together? Who has a needle, who has a pattern and where is a shadow so she can be like everyone else and see her body large and small on the sidewalk? Is she larger in the evening than in the morning and when she eats does she swell up on the spot?*

If she runs and stretches her feet out will the
feet reach back again? Dead, more dead than she
is now, will she die in her sleep? If she smiles, will
the crack in her face widen into a gulf she can climb
back into, can the floor hold her weight? Will the
sky always stay where it is?

Beverly comes to school surrounded by a syrupy-scented per-fume. Under this first candy-coated layer is the urine smell she can't conceal. It trails her everywhere. That's how she knows who she is, how she finds the way back to herself when she has strayed too far. She follows the smell of herself, a hound with its nose to the ground, she sniffs herself out. Here I am, here, here I am.

Puddles under Bev's seat are an everyday event. Her moist clothes stick to her skin and to the chair. Urine is her adhesive.

Kaye and I have stocked up on underwear and jeans for Bev that we keep locked in the teacher's closet. We want to keep her dry and comfortable and to lessen the shame she feels from wetting herself.

As for Eva, she's hunting for as many pictures of people that she can find. Eva cuts them out of magazines and newspapers at game time. She's making a scrapbook of people; she's let them into her world: a man, a boy, a nurse, a mother with her baby. A doctor, a conductor, a garbage collector: the people parade before her and she arranges them into her life.

We now have a speech teacher, Connie, with whom Martin is smitten. Ever since she's arrived, he's been on female alert, waiting and watching for the moment she appears in the classroom to take him for a speech lesson. Martin comes to school carrying invisible bouquets of lilies for her.

These are rare specimens that grow only on
Zagoot: flowers he's cultivated under the direction
of his royal gardener. Just for her.
He has found earth women remarkably knowl-

*edgeable and dazzlingly beautiful, he will kidnap as
many as he can and transport them to Zagoot. Then
he will journey through the stars, returning with
precious stones. A house he will build for them, a
gilded tour de force, and he will have his harem.*

*Dreamily, King Zagoot beams a signal out to his
royal cook. Prepare a feast, a repast of mouthwater-
ing delights upon his forthcoming arrival.*

Unfortunately, the paper on Martin's desk receives no message
at all. It's blank. When Connie, his linguist love, comes into the
room, she takes Ricardo to speech instead of Martin. Martin's chan-
nels get clogged and his armies go berserk.

"Ricardo goes to speech after me! He should not be first. I'm
supposed to be first. I go ahead of Ricardo."

"When you finish what you have to do in here, I'll take you to
speech with me, Martin. I have not forgotten you." Connie's voice
is gentle, yet unwavering.

"Ricardo's going to be shot. My uncle will tear him apart. He's
going to burn. Then we will come into the speech room and freeze
Ricardo."

The tears fall and Martin tries with all his breath to force them
up the gangplank and back into his head. Alas, unsuccessfully.
Nevertheless, Connie's words have impact. He finishes his work,
glancing frequently at the door, awaiting her return and her promise.

November 12

Ricardo builds a volcano in the sand. Beverly copies him. Does
she know what a volcano is? Does Ricardo? Eruptions. His own hot
lava flows, exploding from his insides daily. Hot and searing anger
unleashed on the world, empties out of him. Afterwards he's sullen
and defeated by his outbursts and his inability to hold onto himself. Defeated by all the fault lines he feels inside of him that can't

contain him. The anger inside him swells and swells until it has nowhere to go but outside, pushing and piercing through his hot skin. Nothing can hold it back anymore, he's losing his control. Who and what he is streams out with the anger and he feels empty and afraid.

> *He walks through a barren desert and he hears*
> *his voice like the voice of God jeering at him.*
> *'Come on, come on, come on.' It nabs him on the*
> *chin, elbows him in the ribs, when he strikes back,*
> *no one is there to receive his blows.*
>   *He is shadow boxing in the desert, his horse*
> *is dead, he's sweltering and boiling and there isn't*
> *enough water to quench his thirst. Will he die here*
> *alone with his voice like a thousand cicadas dron-*
> *ing in his mind?*

Martin joins the others. Leaning back on his heels, sorcerer's hat tipped on his head, he summons spirits and poltergeists. Three short whistles, two long ones and he spins around, seven times to the left, seven to the right.

Beverly pokes a hole in Ricardo's volcano. In retaliation, Ricardo grabs all the sand from Beverly's to enlarge his own. He punches her.

"Miss Tina!" A call for help.

"Ricardo and Beverly, it's not right to fight. Miss Tina, they're fighting." Martin calls from ringside. '

"He hit me."

"Aw, you liar, you stupid damn smelly liar."

"Beverly started it, Miss Tina. She spoiled Ricardo's volcano. Didn't you, Beverly?" Martin questions.

"Did not. He bro my volano," Bev slurs the word. "He hit me."

"They are both right. Beverly started first, Miss Tina. Everyone could see that. It's her fault."

I move closer to the sandbox. A volcano is some far off entity.

Something Beverly can't grasp like sand sifting, sifting through her unsure fingers.

"There's enough sand here for everyone. No need to take anyone else's."

To demonstrate, I gather a pile of sand together with my hands. The fight clouds their enjoyment. The three of them stand there and stare into the sand. No one revives the game. Ricardo walks away mumbling to himself and scowls into the floorboards.

"She's a goddamned liar and she knows it." At his desk he slams his books down and bangs his chair into the floor. Playtime is officially over.

The Holiday Spirit

November 22

Pre-Thanksgiving. Our room looks like a butcher shop from colonial America. Cardboard turkeys hang down from the ceiling on strings. Kaye made turkey patterns and everyone received one. Ricardo tore his into feathery bits and released them up into the air, so there's one turkey missing. Beverly colored her turkey black and won't put in the eyes. Today we put on our costumes. Martin comes through the door attired like Captain Smith, wearing his father's belt with a silver buckle on the front and a pair of old army boots. Around his neck are a rose-colored silk scarf and a pair of binoculars. A moustache is penciled in on his upper lip with eye liner. Kaye and I look away from each other to refrain from laughing.

"Good morning, ladies," Captain Smith addresses us.

"Good morning, Martin. How handsome you look," Kaye admires.

"I am Captain Smithy and I thank you." He bows before us.

"Where are the other pilgrims? It's time for our delicious feast!"

"They haven't arrived yet, Captain Smithy. It's too early to eat. That happens at lunch time."

My reality comes from the clock on the wall which reads 9:05. As for Martin's, I'm not sure.

Martin pretends to gnaw on the Indian corn and doesn't forget to wipe his mouth with his pocket handkerchief. The initials M.S. are monogrammed on it. Ricardo comes in wearing a pin-striped bandana on his head. He takes off his shirt. Lipstick is smeared all over his chest. When Martin sees Ricardo's painted flesh he war hoops around him.

"Hi, Chief Uga Muga Ricardo."

"Hi, Captain."

They chase each other around the desks. Ricardo holds the tomahawk Kaye made for him over his head, while he and Martin evoke the gods of harvest. Kaye holds her ears. I will give both of them five minutes of camaraderie and then reinstate the rules. In walks Eva. Two braids hang down her back. Lipstick and rouge on her face, she is dressed in what appears to be a rodeo costume: leather and fringes.

"Pocahontas, you made it!" Martin kisses her hand. Eva giggles, withdraws her hand quickly and smells the anointed kiss. Then over to Ricardo, Eva leans into him and smells the simulated red war paint on his chest.

"Lipstick," Eva comments.

"Ha! Ricardo wears lipstick! Boys don't wear lipstick, only girls wear lipstick. Ricardo wears lipstick." The proverbial battle between the two boys starts up again with Martin's maligning taunt.

"Ricardo's a boy, Eva's a girl," Eva explains to her fingers. Ricardo hits Martin on the head with his cardboard tomahawk. It lacks the impact of his fists, so he kicks him to insure affliction. Martin howls, falls to the floor and takes three minutes to die amid sputtering blood and farewells.

"Okay," I call from my imaginary podium, "time to get in your seats."

Beverly walks in clutching a paper bag. Her knees are bent deeply and her upper torso is pushed down into her hips like a shrunken head.

"What's in the bag?" Eva wants to know.

"My cothum."

Ricardo jerks the bag from Beverly and peeks in. One strand of artificial pearls and he swings it tauntingly around her like a spinning lasso.

"Give it back."

"Aw, this ain't no costume. She don't even have a costume. Lousy, dumb punk." He flings the pearls, just missing her. Beverly covers her face with her arms, grips the pearls, and hides with her head down on the desk.

"Ricardo, that's a terrible way to treat Beverly. Go to the other side of the room and away from her. When you're ready, I expect you to apologize to Bev." He mutters something under his breath and scowls but does as I ask.

"Beverly," I say gently, "we will help you make a costume."

Disbelief. It's only when Kaye cuts the crepe paper, and makes pointed frills around the bottom edges of the skirt, only then does the head look up. Maybe there is something and someone she can believe in after all.

"For me?"

"Yes, it's for you. I need your help. Would you color this?" Beverly stares at Kaye, unable to fully accept the idea that the costume is truly hers.

"Here are the crayons, Bev," I encourage. She won't color; she's fearful that if she does, she might mess it up. This is the first costume she's ever had in her whole life and she's not taking any chances. We work but no one seems able to concentrate. Their minds are into cranberry sauce, turkey giblets, and festivities promised for the afternoon.

We heat up apple cider and serve it with cinnamon sticks. I soaked cloves overnight to soften them, and we make wampum and jewelry by stringing the cloves. Eva pricks her finger and screams.

"Blood, blood, Eva's bleeding." Eva holds her finger in front of her face. "No blood, no blood."

I try to soothe her as we run tap water over the miniscule dots of blood.

"You're okay, Eva. You'll be fine. Let's put a Band-Aid on it."

"Cut. Eva's cut."

"Yes, I know. You'll be all better very soon."

"Eva bleed, Eva die?" Beverly asks.

"No, Bev," I reassure her. "Eva won't die. Eva is fine."

Martin and Ricardo have a powwow in the teepee we've constructed from heavy-duty cardboard. I hear Martin yelp and the teepee falls down on them. Ricardo bangs the teepee and kicks it. He jumps on it and flattens it into the floor.

"What a lousy party this is. This party stinks. Some Thanksgiving this is. This is the worst party ever." Minutes after his tirade in which he verbally trashes the party, the class, his teacher, the school and everything he thinks of about this place, his bus arrives in front of the school.

"Have a nice Thanksgiving, Ricardo," I say to him.

In answer, he throws his tomahawk in the trash and slams the door.

"Gobble, gobble, gobble," Martin's walk resembles a flamingo rather than the turkey he tries to imitate.

On Beverly's sweater, chin, hair, and socks clings the turkey gravy from lunch. When Beverly leaves, she snatches the brown bag from her desk. In it is the costume Kaye told Bev she could keep.

"Bye, Beverly," we call. "Happy Thanksgiving."

"Bye." She waves the hand with the bag in it and smiles.

"And turkey and Coca-Cola and mashed potatoes—." Eva plans her Thanksgiving menu until her bus arrives.

November 25

I love this holiday. For me it is always more special than Christmas. Being with the family is always such a blessing and I don't get to do it enough. I know it's my schedule that keeps me away. Yet, whenever I'm back again with Mom and Dad, Jessie, my younger sister by three years and Stan, the oldest and best brother a girl can have, I realize how good it feels to return to the home I grew up in. This year was no different: a feast fit for kings laid out by Mom. The whole family gathered, laughing, drinking, playing games and catching up. Stan's wife, Colleen is pregnant again with her second child, sex unknown, and Eric, my four year old nephew's wilder than ever. I never saw such activity and enthusiasm rolled up into one kid. He's really sweet and my favorite, not to mention my one and only nephew. How this family got turned onto Scrabble must stem from long tradition. I remember when I was old enough, always playing it at Thanksgiving, along with other board and card games. As a family, we like to laugh and compete affectionately with each other. Invariably, at the end of the evening, the family albums come out. We sit around, sharing memories and stories of our childhood while eating pumpkin and apple pie with vanilla ice cream, laughing and teasing each other. I wish I could bottle up all the extra love that's in the family room and let it loose in my classroom. There's so much to go around, just imagine all the good it would generate.

December 2

I can't quite believe how cold it's turned since the start of the term. The cold seems to catch me unawares: one minute I'm still marveling at the changing colors of fall and the next minute it is deep winter, frigid and unrelenting in its ability to surprise and make daily routines more difficult. Post-Thanksgiving is when there is no denying the wintry truth. Getting out of bed requires some substantial will, even with a warm pair of slippers and a fluffy bathrobe close at hand.

Today I'm also a little bleary-eyed and more in need of morning coffee than usual. I stayed up late last night reading a great science fiction novel by Orson Scott Card. I love when I can get so pulled into a book that the hours just pass and the pages turn and turn. Yet morning still comes with a jolting and unforgiving alarm that shows no mercy on the night owl. Even the soft music of the radio alarm is too intrusive. An espresso for me this morning!

"Ello," Beverly greets me this wintry morning. She is smiling. "Is I a big gel?

"Yes, Beverly, you are a big girl."

"Is you a big gel?"

"I'm a woman."

"Is you bigger than me?"

"Yes, I'm bigger than you."

People come in different sizes and shapes and colors. Beverly pulls her head out of the ground, shedding ostrich feathers on the white sand.

> *She has found her eyes. They were always right on her head, there in front of her all the time. No one reminds her to look there. When the sunlight pours down all warm and comfortable like heavenly homemade applesauce she rubs the crusts of mud and sees a shadow on the ground: A girl's shadow. Is it hers? How does she put it on? Can she jump into it? Leap into it? Must she say a prayer?*
>
> *If she puts it on will she be on the pavement where the shadow is and the shadow where she is up here? Will the shadow walk and talk for her? If she puts it on will it hurt? Will it smell different? Taste different? Will she know it's there? Is she bigger or smaller with the shadow on? Will she be tall or will she just disappear and not be here, evaporate like her urine and not be here at all?*

When Ricardo comes in, he hangs up his coat and sits in his chair, red-eyed and sleepy. I know how he feels; the puffiness has scarcely gone from my own eyes. Whenever we have long vacations, Ricardo comes back dragging his heels. There's always a lot of catching up to do. His good morning greeting is inaudible.

"It's cold in here," the low voice surfaces.

"On Mondays, it is cold in here. You're right about that. Do you have a sweater?"

Ricardo nods.

"Why don't you put it on?" I suggest.

A few moments' hesitation and on goes the sweater. Ricardo shivers in spite of the thick wool wrapped around his body. The gray pullover sweater hangs loosely and looks as if it belonged to an older brother. It could be Fernando's or maybe it belongs to Jose, his oldest brother, now away from home and in the army.

"Why don't you come over here next to me? It's warm by the radiator."

There's something about a cold Monday morning's return after the building has been emptied for a few days. The hot coffee doesn't cut the chill or the overpowering desire to be in bed. I always wear a thicker sweater on Mondays and keep my coffee cup close by to warm my hands around it like a brazier.

"Sleepy?" I ask him as he rubs his eyes.

He nods. My words produce a yawn.

"Good morning, ladies and gentlemen. Brrrr, sure is cold. The gears on my snowmobile are frozen. My father had to drive me to school."

"The bus didn't pick you up this morning, Martin?"

"Nah, somebody hijacked it to the North Pole."

"Well, I hope whoever hijacked the bus brings it back soon so your father doesn't have to drive you every day."

Martin looks at me real strangely for a second. Did he hear me right?

Today Eva is absent. Kaye helps Beverly with her letters. I work with the two boys on math. No one seems able to shake the sleep from their bodies or their eyes. That is, no one but Martin who is totally turbo-powered and brimming over with witticisms and commentary.

December 3

Ricardo looks to see if anyone is watching him. I pretend to be absorbed in my newspaper and watch him from the corner of my eye. Ricardo picks up the doll from the toy chest and flings her across the rug. Again he lifts up her rubbery body and bangs it to the floor. Is he imitating his brother who always picks on him and assaults him when their parents are out of reach? Mrs. Ricardo told me that she's worried, but can't seem to stop it, and Mr. Ricardo isn't home a lot to intervene.

"I'll smash you. Smash you! You hear me?"

December 10

Beverly's favorite expression for everyone is 'bones.' She asks question after question in search of her skeletal identity. Questions about the size and shape of people, especially her, where her organs are, will her bones break and will she die if she falls. The questions are Bev's way of negotiating her world and making sense of it and making sense of her. She's finding herself, fitting the puzzle pieces of herself together and learning to be her own person and not her mother. Anthropologist and archeologist, her self-discoveries are more frequent events that we applaud and encourage.

"Is she bigga 'n me?"

"Eva is taller and older than you are, Bev."

"How old I is?"

"Seven years old." I count up to seven and display seven fingers.

"Is you older than me?

"Yes, Bev, I'm older than you are."

"I'm bad," she confides, whispering into her hand.

"Who said you're bad?"

"My mommy."

"Why did she tell you that?"

"'Cause I got into the peanut butter."

"Maybe you did something that you weren't supposed to do, something your mother felt was wrong."

"Is you think I is bad?"

"No, Beverly, I don't think you're bad. I think you're nice. A nice brown-eyed, brown-haired girl and what pretty dimples you have."

Beverly laughs and hugs me. Did I say hug? I mean presses and squeeze-dries. Her legs are wrapped around my ankles and I am compressed by her sudden outflowing of appreciation. I am her ancestral link to herself, a primordial appendage. If she carries my body around with her, or more accurately, if I lug her tenacious bundle of muscles and cells and bones, will life be easier? Not for me. Beverly is no featherweight.

"You want to see your dimples?"

I spin us around, her feet clamp on tighter and she hangs on. At the mirror, which is nailed to the door, we look at two faces. I show Beverly her dimpled cheeks.

"Is you got dimples?"

"Yup. See?" Together we gaze at the infinite wonders of Homo sapiens.

"We're going to Christmas tomorrow," Eva declares.

Eva would like Christmas to come every other day. In the long interval between Christmases, Eva will schedule birthdays. Every day is a monumental event, and Eva expects homage dutifully delivered like a newspaper service: Sunday through Sunday. Bring it to her home address, school address or her celestial one in the form of presents. Only presents are to be sacrificed to the priestess.

"No, Eva, not yet. Tomorrow is not Christmas. We have some time before the Christmas holiday. But Christmas will be here soon."

"I want Christmas," Eva wails. "I want Christmas."

"I want Christmas, too," I say, envisioning days of quiet respite. "We have to wait. I know it's hard to wait."

"I want Christ-m-a-a-s!" Eva kicks her chair and throws her work paper around. Presents are propitious, not promises.

"Well, well, what have we here?" Master Martin is called in to preside at the inquisition. "Eva Kineva, Eva Kineva."

"No, Eva Kineva, no Eva!" she shrieks."

Martin holds out his toreador cape, and Eva lunges at him in Technicolor red.

"Hold it, hold it. Calm down."

Martin backs away, shaken by the deadpan face of his playmate, not to mention the brutish-looking spikes of her teeth.

"Christmas is coming, Santa is coming," Martin sings.

"Christmas?" she sniffles, looking at Martin. "Take me to Christmas."

"All right. Let's go." He grabs Eva's hand and revs up his time machine. "Rrrrrruuum, rrrumnun. Verrrruuummm!"

"No." Eva rushes off, leaving Martin in between yesterday and tomorrow.

"Eva," Miss Kaye calls, "let's make a list of things you want Santa to bring you." Kaye takes out a long sheet of construction paper. Eva's lists are hanging all over the walls. There are at least two notebooks full in her desk. Soon we will have to move the class out of the room. Christmas present lists are filling in for people.

Mayhem and Mistletoe

December 20

When I woke up and saw that it was a gray blustery day, I should have trusted the signs and spent the day in hibernation. My bed was feeling so soft and cozy I didn't want to leave the warmth of the comforter and the flannel sheets. No matter how piercingly loud the alarm was, I kept pushing down on the radio snooze button to buy myself more time until the last possible moment. Even then it was a struggle to leave the apartment and I barely made it to work on time.

Today is our trip to Center City Philadelphia, Gimbels department store, and a visit to see Santa. Approaching the school building, I spy a small cat wandering around the school grounds. Naturally I carry him up to our room.

"Where are you going with that?" Rita asks as she sees me sneaking up the steps.

"Shhh." I wink.

"What next?" Her hands are raised in a gesture of despair, but the wink is returned.

"Is him a cat?" Beverly points to the furry animal in my arms.

"Yes." I put the cat down. "Do you know what these are?"

"Hair?"

"Like hair, they're whiskers. You're a smart girl, Beverly. Look. He's licking himself all over. That's how he takes a bath. He cleans himself with his tongue."

"Oh, no, Tina," Kaye moans when she sees our visitor. "What are you up to now?" And in the same breath, "I'll be back with some milk."

"I loves him," Bev coos. "I wants him to loves me. Does he loves me?"

"He has to get to know you first. Right now, he's a little afraid." Kaye returns with milk and a bowl.

"You are resourceful today," I smile at Kaye.

"I 'borrowed' it." Her polite way of saying it's ours eternally.

"Are we goin'?" Ricardo questions as he walks through the door. He looks doubtful. All braced up for postponement and lost promises.

"Of course we're going," Kaye exclaims. "Did you think we were only fooling?"

"Nah," he says sheepishly.

Eva has a paper bag containing the essential lists for Santa — the ones she wants to arrive at the door first. She's hoping she can turn on her feminine charm and take some loot home with her at Santa's request.

> *If she's lucky she can haul the entire toy department into a U-Haul van she will park illegally outside Gimbels. She doesn't have a driver's license; she rips up parking tickets or has them fixed by her cousin Alec, who is Earth Commissioner. She will have Ricardo drive the van and Martin will direct traffic while they load and unload the goods. Beverly will help her hold the door as the workmen she's flown down from Venus float out the store.*

The kitten laps up the milk, aware of watchful eyes from every direction. Where is Martin?

"Okay," I put on my authoritative voice. "There are some rules. We have to stay together so we don't get lost or hurt. And we must have partners." I address the troops with the microphone switched off. "No fighting, no pushing, et cetera."

Eva's fingers tap 'et cetera' in the air. What is this unfamiliar earth word?

"Am I late?" Martin bursts through the door wearing his London Fog with the collar pushed up against his neck and carrying a black umbrella concealed in his coat like a weapon.

"Whew, sorry to keep you ladies waiting," Martin bows in front of Kaye and me. "I had a very important case to investigate."

"What happened?" I am always interested in learning more about the secret life of Martin Selby: intrigue and illusion.

"On Jupiter, where I spent the night, no one had phone dials. There was only one person who did, but he never returned from his mission—Mission Night Owl. The natives are angry. They almost missed the shower commercial. Look out!" He draws out his umbrella. "Stay where you are. Don't anyone move."

I raise my hands in the air slowly. This is a hold-up, and I'm glad I don't carry my jewels or my artwork.

"Hold it. Breathe only if you must. Drop your weapons or I'll shoot."

I drop my imaginary pistol and freeze. Ricardo pounces on Martin's back from behind.

"Ricardo, stop it! You're not supposed to do that. You are not allowed to do that. You will be ripped apart by a leopard. A tiger will eat your head off. Ow! Stop it, stop it!" he squeals.

"Okay, Ricardo, get down. We have a lot to do if we want to go on our trip."

"Yeah, you're just sayin' that 'cause you know we're not going. That's what you mean, we're not goin'." Ricardo jumps down and Martin spars with a microscopic opponent.

"We're going to Christmas, we're going to Christmas," Eva sings happily.

Coats and umbrellas. Keys. A mass exodus and one squirming kitten in my arms. We wave goodbye to Rita as we pass the office. The door opens and there in living color is our world. Beverly gives the kitten a cast iron hug, and I set him on the wet cement. The misguided cat cries and follows us.

"Oh, no," Kaye whispers, "Now you've done it." A car and a cat are about to approach the street simultaneously. Kaye picks up the cat and escorts him across the street.

"Him loves us," Bev deduces as the cat watches our departure.

Our bus arrives and we bump towards the city. A short one-block walk and Gimbels is before us like an oasis. The first announcement, at 10:45, is from Ricardo.

"I'm hungry."

We are in the midst of a gourmet palace in the shopping area. Fast food service includes everything edible from a sprout health salad to chili. Kaye and I are tantalized by the smells, and my internal caloric meter blows a fuse.

"Well, Kaye, do you want to eat?"

"Right!" She is emphatic.

Beverly with her palate 'extraordinaire,' wants a hot dog from the delicatessen vendors. Ricardo grudgingly munches a soggy egg salad sandwich he's pulled from his lunchbox and picks out invisible pieces of eggshell. We tell him he can have a hot dog too, and the storm clouds clear momentarily. Give Eva anything, but make it edible and fragrant. We are sitting at a table, watching the rush of human traffic walk by us. Children and their mothers, couples, and college students are all gearing up for the holidays, arms loaded down with shopping bags and presents. Everyone in our crew is busy and noisily chomping on the hotdogs we've purchased. Everyone that is, but Martin. No, Martin does not eat earth food.

> *He has not had a chance to send samples for analysis to the lab on Zagoot. The King was warned that earthlings put chemicals in their food that would kill one Zagootian bird in less than three minutes. Zagootians don't die easy. And King Zagoot never dies. He will live on forever and ever.*

After filling our bellies, we ride up the escalator to find Santa. Ricardo sees Santa and dodges other people to run ahead of us. Luckily, there is only one boy ahead of Ricardo.

"And what do you want?" the red-costumed gentleman asks Ricardo.

"A car." Face to face with the awesome Santa, Ricardo's voice is small.

"What else do you want?"

"I don't know."

"A truck?" Santa coaches.

"Yeah."

Eva's next. Rather than read the endless lists, she folds the papers into his hand along with her address and some stamps in case Santa is short of postage or reindeer or in need of clarification. Before she hops down from the platform, she sniffs his beard, his moustache, and checks his pockets to see if there are any pre-Christmas give-aways. There aren't.

"What would you like for Christmas, little girl?" Santa asks Beverly.

"I is a big gel." Some things Beverly does learn fast.

"What do you want, big girl?"

"Uh, a car, a truck," she borrows Ricardo's choices.

Santa seemed pleased with that. He didn't scold or yell at Ricardo. Nothing happened to Ricardo after he said that. He's still here, still all right. He didn't die.

Now, what could Santa possibly give the great magician that he can't already give to himself? Martin wonders. He asks for a laser beam gun, an electronics set, and a two-wheeler because he doesn't want Santa to feel bad.

Downstairs is—you guessed it—another Santa Claus. How do I explain who the real Santa is? A pair of roller skates transports the cherry-blossomed gentleman from the second to the first floor. No one minds at all. Beverly's in ecstasy. This Santa not only talks, he gives away candy canes. Bless you, Santa.

Eva, Beverly and I go to the ladies room. When we exit, we

see a crowd gather where Kaye and the rest of the children are. As we approach, I hear Ricardo's screams. I move in for a closer look, ready to act if necessary. Is he hurt? There on the floor of Gimbels department store is Ricardo, thrashing around wildly and uncontrollably. Kaye's trying to hold his feet and hands so he doesn't injure her and so she doesn't hurt him. Although we use it sparingly, proper restraint is an approved technique in his IEP. I'm remembering what the personnel from his former school wrote in his file. They said that Ricardo was violent and dangerous. Are we about to witness that Ricardo and get a real sample of his extreme behavior? He's been aggressive, yes, but never the way the file notes read.

"Get off me, you motherfucker. Get your damned hands off me."

"Not until you settle down. I'm not going to let you hurt me or anyone else," Kaye's voice is calm, repeating the words we say over and over to him, while ignoring his cursing.

"Oh yeah?" Ricardo tries to kick his feet, but Kaye has them in a secure hold. A policeman appears. Martin is jubilant; he salutes and clicks his heels together, fascist fashion.

"Do you need any help?" the policeman asks me.

"No." How to explain that this is all part of a normal day's work routine?

"Okay," the policeman booms. "Now everyone, please just move along," he says to the curious bystanders gathered around us. I'm at Kaye's side. Ricardo is panting and tries to wriggle himself free from Kaye's grip.

"Ricardo, as soon as you calm down you can get up. Let's settle down a little bit."

A lady from the crowd screams at him, "Now, Ricardo, stop that right now and behave." In surprise, we turn to the strange lady. My sense of protection rears up.

"Excuse me ma'am, but please don't interfere. I know you mean well but your words aren't helping us to calm him down." She stares strangely at me and turns dismissively.

"Now, what's your name and telephone number, miss?" Martin asks, hot on the heels of the retreating woman. "We need to know this information. You are a Number One Witness, and we may need to contact you. This fellow is very dangerous. Who knows when he'll strike again?" He pulls a pad and pencil from the atmosphere and jots down a description of the woman.

"Mar-tin," I shout. "Over here, now!"

The woman's intervention, the crowd and the policeman sober Ricardo. He gets up. All the lights, the Christmas decorations and two Santa Clauses have overstimulated him. Christmas is beginning to take on a dissonant strain. Outside there's a heavy downpour of rain.

"Wow, did you see that policeman?" Martin asks. Kaye nods. No one feels much like talking. No one, that is, but Martin.

"Ricardo, why don't you put your hat on?" my maternal voice. "You're getting soaked."

"I don't care. I want to get wet."

> *Real wet with pneumonia till he has to stay in bed and no one knows if he'll live or die. And his mother's crying and his father brings him racing car magazines and his brother lets him hold onto his pocket knife. He gets real sick and he has to have his meals in bed and a TV set in his room. And maybe he doesn't die. Just, maybe.*

The bus comes and Ricardo doesn't move. I grab his hand.

"Ow, you're holding it too tight, let go," he screams. However, the hand does not pull away from my grip. Somehow we board the bus and I sit down next to him.

"Don't sit by me. Get away from me. I'm sitting alone."

"Ricardo," I say, in a controlled but weary voice, "I'm sitting here. I'm not moving. I won't look at you. You don't have to talk to me. In fact, I don't want you to."

"You're not sitting here. Get out of here." Ricardo turns toward the window. We sit next to each other in a thick silence.

At school, Ricardo refuses to come inside the room. He stands outside, his arms across his chest doing the hall shuffle with his feet.

"You know something, Kaye?" I confide. "I'm exhausted."

"I don't see why. We've had such a relaxing day!"

Beverly's asleep on the rug. The others leave when their buses arrive and I close my eyes and pretend just for a moment that I never got out of bed.

December 23

We make popcorn to string on our Christmas tree. I take out the electric burner which I've brought from home and take advantage of their excitement to teach a lesson. It engages their senses and is an experiential and viable learning opportunity. Everyone gathers around the table. Eva spoons the oil into the pot; Ricardo pours the yellow kernels of corn we've measured. Martin. Martin bursts into tears.

"I want to put the popcorn in the pot. I want to do it. You won't let me. I want to do it now! You're a bad woman. My father hates you. My father will send you away."

"Martin, you can shake the pan to make the popcorn pop," I suggest.

"No, I want to put in the popcorn. And now it's too late. I don't want to do anything else."

"Okay, I'll give someone else that job."

"Nooo! I'll do it," he sniffles.

"It popping, it popping," Beverly jumps up and down.

> *The floor does not cave in. She looks down and*
> *sees her toes all wriggly, toes and feet and ankles*
> *and knees. When she touches them, they do not fall*
> *off, they do not bleed. She is salmon-colored like her*

sweater, softer than her sweater, made of flesh that
doesn't char in the night, and that howls in her pil-
low.
　　There are skeletons under her bed that clatter
when she moves. She rides out the storm of her wheez-
ing breath in a cradle carved from decaying bones.

We watch the oil bubble; we listen for the popping. The kernels, geysers of yellow corn, explode. More go into our mouths than on the strings. Ricardo races to finish first. Are there any contenders? Within his deft fingers, the popped corn crumbles and tumbles off the string. He tosses the popcorn, string, and needle into the air. Ricardo stomps back to his lone desk, pulling his hood over his head and burying his face in his arms.

"What's the matter, Ricardo?"

"It's no good, it's not right."

"Would you like to try again? Do you want some help?" Kaye questions.

With his head still tucked, his body shakes with quiet weeping. The other children hang theirs on the tree. Eva hops over to Ricardo, sniffs him and lightly touches his bent back. No kicks, no punches in return. The blessing is received in humility.

"Ricardo," Eva says. Do sadness and defeat have a particular scent, I wonder.

"How would you like to help me pick up the lunches, Ricardo?" I ask him as the hour draws closer to lunch time.

Martin and Beverly play with the dolls in the back. Eva makes a basket for the popcorn that she's saving to take home.

"For the tree," she whispers to the scissors and scotch tape.

Ricardo doesn't reply. He draws himself out of his seat, slow and easy.

　　It's a showdown. His hands rest on his holster,
ready to spring. His fingers are hot and tingling

pressed up against the trigger, he eases along with
his legs in a wide 'v'.

His head is bent; he can feel the metallic weight
of the gun against his thigh pushing into him heavy
and hard. Once a comfort and a necessary append-
age for survival, to keep him safe and keep him
strong, the gun feels like it no longer belongs.

I wait at the door for him and we walk to the lunchroom. On the way up the stairs, laden with plastic cartons, Ricardo peeks at me from behind a plastic wrapped cheeseburger. "If I'm still hungry, can I get another lunch?"

"If you're hungry, of course we'll get you another one."

Today is early dismissal and everyone has celebration and vacation on their minds. The class phone rings loudly to alert us that the buses are downstairs.

"Have a wonderful holiday," I call to the bustling coats, gloves, hats and earmuffs (who else but Martin) on their way out the door.

"Well, Tina," Kaye sighs, "I'm going to spend Christmas doing nothing but having a good time."

"Have a nice vacation, Kaye. And a good rest; you deserve it. I'm going to see my family but still have some Christmas shopping to do." We hug and leave our room behind us for ten whole days!

'Twas the night before Christmas and all through
the house, the only creature stirring was Martin
Mouse. Hanging up his Santa-traps of fish net and
rope and watching for Santa to slide down the slope.

He will capture mighty Santa and bring him to his
knees, whisk him to Planet Zagoot in less time than
a sneeze. Zagootians will line up in unearthly delight
and as Santa gives out presents there's never a fight.

Zagootians are trained, indeed taught, to live well
by their King's noble edict: 'More Heaven than Hell.'

New Resolve

January 3

"How was your Christmas vacation, Ricardo?" Kaye asks.

"I didn't have no Christmas. Santa didn't come to my house."

"My father had frozen orange juice. He was crying in his glass of frozen orange juice and it was cold," sings Martin.

How do I make sense of this verbiage? I know Mr. and Mrs. Selby have been having marital problems because she's confided in me. Martin isn't handling his parents' conflict very well. Mr. Selby has a hard time adjusting to Martin's behavior, his diverse characters and fanciful imagination, but that can't be the sole reason for their difficulties. I know it's not easy for them. Martin can be exhausting.

Ricardo won't work. He sits underneath his desk; his pencil scratches along the floor. I won't push today. I don't know what his vacation was like but from the way he's acting, it wasn't merry.

"Calling all cars, calling all cars. Red car alert. Now hear this. Beverly Crimp is a thief. She's loose. Don't let her escape!" Martin removes the snow goggles he's been wearing all morning to protect his delicate membranes from the two feet of imaginary glaring snow layered on the classroom floor. He chases Beverly and she giggles.

"Stop, I say stop! Thief. You will stop, now!" Martin cautions.

"I is not, Martin."

"Oh yes you are and we will get you."

"Beverly, if you want something, why don't you just ask me for it first? If I can, I'll give you what you want. I'd like you to ask me."

"Is I punit?"

"No, Beverly," I reply, "you're not punished, but you will have to give all the crayons back. You can't keep them."

When she sees in the darkness, she climbs up the stairs brushing bugs and cobwebs from her arms and face as they bump against her. There's a room in the attic, a chest in the attic. Her fingers stumble with the rusty lock; she pries it open with her teeth.

Inside the chest is a linen wedding dress. She smooths out the wrinkles with her fingers and puts the dress on. She dances to the orange moon draped low in the starless sky.

The moon turns blood red and splatters against the attic window. She looks down at the dress stained with red splotches, the dress won't come off. The dress won't come loose and there is warm blood caking under her fingernails.

When the moon falls from the sky and the window whistles and screams in the wind, no one hears her calls for help in the attic.

January 10

"Has anyone seen my black magic marker?" Kaye inquires. "That's funny. I thought I put it right here in the drawer." She searches.

"She's got it. She's the one," Martin points an accusing yellow banana at Beverly.

"I's do not."

"Oh yeah?" Ricardo growls. He's crouched down by her desk, pulling everything out. Pencils, paper clips, dice, Martin's baby picture, Eva's tarot cards, a black magic marker, even a crushed and moldy peanut butter sandwich falls to the floor.

"Beverly, did you take Kaye's magic marker?"

"Noooo."

"How did it get in your desk?"

"I don' oo."

"She did too take it. She takes everything. Her smelly fingers steal everything," Ricardo accuses.

"It's not right to steal, Beverly," Martin warns. "You'll be punished. You will be hanged." Martin constructs an imaginary gallows from the jump rope and ties a noose on one end. He slips a doll's head in the noose. The doll is hung five consecutive times by Martin and stoned with the bean bags Ricardo hurls at the doll's drooping body.

"Tell the weather man to turn off all the snow, Miss Tina; it's cold in Marlboro country."

"I'll see what I can do, Martin. Now finish your work, please."

Eva's dad is standing at the door, and Eva's body is flapping behind him.

"I had to bring her to school. The bus didn't come and an older girl attacked her while she was waiting at the bus stop."

"Eva, are you all right? Is she all right?"

"Yes, she is. Just a little upset. I think she's more frightened than hurt."

"All right. All right. Upset." Eva's bottom lip is puffy and her fingers angrily thump the air. She is dazed. The echolalia is worse than it's been in some time. When I lead her inside the classroom, she won't sit down and whirls around and around on one foot like a rotisserie. Kaye wraps her arm protectively around Eva's shoulders.

"Mr. Turner, Miss Kaye will take Eva to the nurse and the nurse will check to make sure Eva's all right. We'll let you know how she is later on in the day. It's not necessary for you to wait if you need to get to work, please go ahead, we'll see that she's okay, won't we Eva?"

"Well, I really do have to get to work. I just don't like to leave her when she's in such a state like this. She's been doing so well and talking and relating to us more. It's like having our little girl with us.

I don't understand how some children can be so violent and down-right cruel. I just don't understand." Mr. Turner pushes his eyeglass frames up against the bridge of his nose, swallows hard to check his feelings and then recomposes himself.

"I'll call you from the office later on to see how Eva's doing. Thank you for everything you're doing for our daughter."

"You're very welcome, Mr. Turner," I answer.

He turns to Eva, "I'll see you after school, Eva, Okay? Miss Tina and Miss Kaye are going to take care of you. Mommy and I will see you tonight."

"Take care, Mr. Turner and thank you for bringing Eva to school. We'll talk later on. I'm sure she'll be just fine as she settles into our routine," I smile and he nods.

He kisses his subdued daughter on her forehead before leaving.

"What happened to her?" Ricardo questions.

"A girl hurt her while she was waiting for the bus."

"I wish I was there. I wudda smashed them. Yeah, I wudda given her such a fat lip."

"That's what happens when people fight. Right, Miss Tina?"

"Right, Martin."

"Aw, I wudda punched that girl's nose in so bad she'da been all bloody." Ricardo is bruising for a fight.

"Yeah, and I will poison her with my poison dart machine and drown her in the Red Sea and throw her off a mountain in the Swiss Chocolate Alps," Martin pipes up.

"Is her gonna die?" Bev asks me.

"No, Bev, Eva is not going to die."

Eva and Kaye return. An ice pack is on Eva's lips. Everyone comes over to investigate and stick their fingers on the cold pack. Eva rests her head on the desk.

She is waiting outside the temple, a crown of garlands in her long silky hair, as she inhales frank-incense and counts out the passing minutes on her rosary fingers. Soon the oracle will see her, for on her willowy back she carries a flurry of messages.

The townspeople steal her flowers and replace them with pointed thorns. They roll barrels of thunder to chase her down a steep mountain and she falls deep into a ravine. She washes the wounds in the cool stream and gazes wistfully upon her slippery reflection.

"Hurts, Eva hurts," she whispers to her fingers.

"I know Eva hurts. Eva will be all right," I assure her as Martin folds his parka like a pillow and lends it to Eva.

King Zagoot shoots his flare gun up to Zagoot and contacts his adviser for personal affairs. Assemble the Zagootians; have them prepare for his return. Tell them to take showers or baths depending on their lottery numbers and take care to wash behind their ears and under their arms.

Call in the royal cook and instruct him to prepare for a wedding banquet. Call in the royal priest and he and his future queen will zagoot up faster than you can say Eva Kineva.

January 26

"What color is this, Beverly?"

"I don' oo."

"Sure you do. What color is it?"

"It red?"

"Is it red, Beverly?"

"Les, it red."

"And you are right! See you do know. I knew you could tell me." Beverly grins.

*She puts on the glasses and peers through the
lenses. The doll's face is rose-colored, the Jell-O
she slurps off the spoon is strawberry red and Eva's
dress, the one she wore to school yesterday, is fire
engine red.*

*Lollipop red is her favorite. When she grows
up she will brush her lips ruby red: like a princess
she'll go to the ball. Red, red, it's not all the time
now that she wets the bed. And sometimes she feels
more alive than dead.*

"Dear Mrs. Luciano, Ricardo's a bad boy. He made cherry bombs in school, and the principal told him, 'You're a bad boy.' And now he's kicked out of school, and he can't go back no more. We are very sorry."

I record as Ricardo dictates. "Is there anything else you want me to write down?"

"Nah."

"What do you want me to do with the paper?" I ask.

"I dunno. Keep it in your desk till we need it."

"When do you think we'll need it?"

"Sometime, maybe."

"Okay, we'll keep it until then, right here." He watches me put the letter in the desk drawer. Maybe this is the missing information that's not in his files: Ricardo's incendiary exploits. Thank goodness, they're behind him! The best news is that he's sorry for his past misconduct.

In the afternoon the classroom is transformed into a French kitchen about forty kilometers from the outskirts of Nice. Yes, we're cooking and everyone gets into the act with drama and props that would outdo any live stage performance. Throughout it all, we're still learning measurements, reading, following directions, sharing and cooperating. Yet at the same time, we depart a little from ourselves and our lives and engage in playful experience that's instructive, therapeutic, and builds character and sociability. And fun. That's one of the goals I've set for my class. These kids are to have fun learning. None of their experiences with education has been especially positive so far. I want them to unlearn some of their negative associations with school and instruction. It's hard on kids who don't fit the standard mold. I hope I can be instrumental in bringing out the best in these children and help them to have more positive experiences in the future. Eva seems to be well on the way to embracing learning and engaging with it fully and this is great. Watching each child's successes and improvements, no matter how small, lifts my heart on a daily basis. They are amazing.

Martin dons his chef's hat. Eva ties a white apron around her waist and puts a net over her hair like she has seen grandma do. Of course, Beverly wants an apron too, so she puts hers on, inside out and upside down. Ricardo tries to juggle the wooden spoons while balancing an apple on his nose. Kaye and I hand out the rest of the apples and the Tupperware that I brought from home. Everyone unwraps the caramels.

"Hey, she's eating them all," Ricardo's voice is menacing. "She's gonna eat them all up. Cut it out, ya little jerk." He kicks Bev under the table.

"I ain't." Bev's mouth is so full of caramel goo it barely opens. Her upper and lower molars are stuck together and she's swallowed her tongue, thinking it was the softest piece of caramel she's ever bitten into.

"Beverly and everybody, listen up. If we eat all the caramels now, we won't have any caramels to dip our apples into."

"She had some. We all get in trouble; it's that little dummy's fault."

"Ricardo, you're not in trouble. No one's in trouble. While we're working we can have three caramels each. Beverly, you had yours."

"Three! I bet she had twenty." Ricardo pops his three into his mouth and kicks the table.

"If you bump the table like that, something might break. I'd like you to stop now so no one gets hurt."

My voice is a little grainier than usual. I see an accident waiting to happen if he loses control and overturns the table or worse. I envision hot caramel sauce oozing into someone's unsuspecting lap. The vision's not a pretty one. For safety's sake, I must act fast and judiciously so that Ricardo's anger doesn't flare up.

"Aw, you don't care about me."

"I care about everyone in here." My voice is calm and I smooth down the plastic tablecloth on the other side of the table with both hands, just in case I have to exert physical strength to keep it steady.

"Nah, you don't. You just care about those dumb bitches." Ricardo storms away from the table and pushes his desk. He sits on the windowsill with his back turned to us and ties the cords on the shades into tight knots.

"I hate this place. I ain't never comin' back to this hole."

"Well, you can stay over there for a while anyway, Ricardo, because that's not how to talk to girls or to anyone. They deserve your respect."

"It's melting, Miss Tina," Martin informs me.

When Martin graduates from this class, he's accepted a scholarship to apprentice with an internationally acclaimed clique of chefs in Geneva. His future is sealed. He and I lay wax paper out on the table, and everyone gets a chance to roll their apples in caramel glop.

"Hey, where's mine?" Ricardo's voice is soft again, the way it is when he's quiet and sorry, but can't outwardly apologize.

> *He crawls out of the foxhole and saunters over*
> *to the bar where his company is toasting victory.*
> *He's covered in dust and sweat and is ready for*
> *something to wash out the sediment he feels in his*
> *mouth and the loneliness he feels all over.*

"Your apple is right here waiting for you, Ricardo. We didn't forget about you; we saved you one. Dip it in while the caramel's still hot."

"Mmm, this is deee-licious," Martin pays an earthling the highest compliment.

February 2

"Open the door, Miss Tina!" Eva calls out.

"You're going to have to get some strength in those fingers," I tease.

"Strength in those fingers," Eva repeats and giggles. "How do you spell 'kitchen'?"

"K-i-t-c-h-e-n."

"How do you spell grandmother?"

Words go up on the board. Eva calls them out faster than I can write them.

"Spell Martian, Miss Tina." Martin talks into his microphone. "Spell Zagoot."

'Zagoot' is visible in yellow chalk. Martin is quiet for two glorious seconds and then laughs.

> *King Zagoot has told the Zagootians about a faraway place called 'earth.' The little Zagootians want to visit.*
>
> *He's going to zagoot them to earth, but first they must learn about earth in their history lessons so they are knowledgeable and will not disgrace their king, who is well versed in seven planetary languages. He is arduously studying the eighth. He finds Earthlingese so esoteric, even for him.*

I'm impressed that more of Martin's imaginary characters are surfacing and he's comfortable enough to share his inner world with us and speak about them aloud. This is progress for him and for all of us.

February 6

"I'm 'hipractic,'" Ricardo confesses.

"You're what?" I want to be sure I heard him correctly.

"Hipractic. *You* know," Ricardo repeats.

"What does it mean?"

"It means wild."

"Oh, hyperactive. Who said that you were hyperactive?"

"That's what they called me at my other school I used to go to, but they kicked me out."

"There are times when we're all hyperactive. It means when we have a lot of energy: Too much for our own good, sometimes. Like when you're in a rush and accidentally knock something down. All that hurrying is hyperactive. And then there are times when we are slow and sticky like molasses."

Ricardo looks up and smiles weakly.

"Gooey Ricardo, gooey Ricardo," Martin laughs.

"Gooey Martin, gooey Martin," Ricardo retorts.

"Gooey Beverly, gooey Beverly." Martin pulls the imaginary salt water taffy off Ricardo's fingers and flings it in Beverly's face and both boys laugh loudly. I reprimand them.

Despite Ricardo's anger and left-out feelings, he's really looking at his behavior now and at what happened at his other school. The massive reports I've read of all the trouble and mayhem that he caused previously are astounding. He doesn't seem like that same kid. I know he's prone to outbursts and confrontation, but something is changing, even if it's really subtle. He seems more ready to accept what he's done in the past and maybe a little remorseful. At the same time, he wants so much to be accepted and not seen as some wild creature. He may not know how to go about getting it, but he's aching for love and acceptance. It's a craving of his that never leaves. I'm hoping that with a loving atmosphere of trust and support which this class is, he'll be able to feed what's lacking and feel whole.

Angels, Demons and Mister X

February 7

"Tasha is pretty."

Tasha is a girl who rides on Bev's bus. I know the little girl; she's in second grade and has cute pigtails and big brown eyes.

"So is Beverly," I assure her.

"Is I'm pretty?"

"Yes, you are. I think you're pretty."

"You loves me?"

"Yes, Beverly, I love you."

"My mommy don't loves me."

"Oh, that's not true, Bev. I know she loves you very much."

> *When the night creeps silently away, she sweeps*
> *the starry sleep from her eyes. She climbs out of*
> *her creaking bed and dresses herself in gold-spun*
> *raiment. Into the hallway of mirrors she wanders,*
> *blowing the dust powder off her fingers.*
>
> *There in the silver looking glass she stares at the*
> *image of herself. The mirror holds open its arms as*
> *wide as the dawn and she tiptoes inside.*

"Look, Ricardo, it's time to get to work. Now settle down and get it done."

"Yeah, well I ain't gonna do nothin' in here no more. I'm sick of you always tellin' me what to do. What d'ya think, I'm your slave or somethin'? I ain't your slave."

Two steps forward, one step back or the other way around I think, as I brace myself for one of his explosions. Was I kidding myself when I thought we were making progress here? No time for doubts; I watch Ricardo carefully.

His chair slams into the floor and he crashes out of the room, leaving papers flying in his wake. Once outside of the room, he pummels the door with his fists. I go after him. When he sees me following, he slides against the wall away from me, folds his arms tightly across his chest and furrows his brow. Pouting, he actually looks very endearing and comical in his attempt to be threatening and my eyes soften as I mask a smile.

"Ricardo, I'd like to talk to you."

Hands pressed to his ears, he shuts out my words.

"When I raise my voice sometimes, it doesn't mean that I don't care about you. I do care about you. Even when I'm angry with you, I still care about you. That doesn't change." My voice floats off and diffuses through the fan of his fingers. "I'm going back inside now. When you're ready I'd like you to come back and finish your work." I watch him from the open door.

"Miss Tina, want to hear me read in this book?" Martin greets me.

"Sure I do. Just let me catch my breath." I reach in the air for it, but my breath is lingering outside sighing in Ricardo's ear. I shrug.

"Here it is," and, out of all the places, Martin pulls it out of his back pocket and throws it to me.

"Thanks," I say as I catch my breath before it hits the floor. "Now let's hear you read."

And Martin begins: "Once there was a little boy who tied fire-crackers of courage onto his ankles and blindfolded his eyes. He was afraid, so he asked someone else to fire them up. His insides exploded and he threw away the earmuffs so he could find where his insides were crying."

"Martin, you read beautifully and the story is certainly very interesting. I have a new book to give you, one like Eva's. Would you like that?"

"Well, now, let me think. Hmmm. I really need to consult with Mister X about this but he's at a very important meeting. Now I must reach him. I got it! I'll fly him in my helicopter mobile pronto to talk it over, Miss Tina."

"All right Martin. When he arrives, let me know what you and he decide and then I can give you the book if you'd like."

Martin's mention of Mister X is more frequent. It's as though he wants his inner and external worlds to merge and not be so separate. I realize how much courage that must take. Mrs. Selby clued me in a while ago about Martin's entourage of friends. Martin plays many different characters throughout a day and confers with invisible ones. It's only recently that he refers to more of them directly. I take the introduction as a compliment and indicative of our growing trust. I watch as imagination, play, and the secret world of Mr. Martin dance and tumble together in the unfolding dramatic scene.

Martin and Mister X quibble over travel expenses. Mister X is huffy and forgets his head, leaving it squawking on Martin's desk. It doesn't worry Martin. He knows Mister X will come back for it. He has to. Joyously he thinks of all the money he's saving. Ricardo steps into the classroom after watching the scene from the hallway, and plays into the game with his own personal twist. He walks over to Martin and bows, pretending to carry Mister X's hat in his hand.

"Here you are, my man."

"Why thank you kind sir. You are the man; yes indeedy!" He turns to me.

"Miss Tina, I'm honored to say yes." Martin bows to the east and to the west. He bows to Eva.

"How do you spell Martin?" Eva's interest piques at Martin's attention.

February 8

Kaye busily decorates the room like Disney World. Cartoon characters stand on the wall holding letters and numerals, waiting to step out of their picture frame poses and come alive. Apparently they've solicited Martin, and he's agreed to become their press agent provided he plays the leading role in all productions. Yet right now, he scans the room and takes us all in while we're busy with our separate tasks.

"Hold it. Stand right where you are." Martin's photographic eye surveys the tableau through the imaginary lens of his movie camera. "Alrighty, now. Everybody do just what you are doing but smile. Smile."

"Thank you, Martin. Is my smile on straight? And how about my makeup, does it need touching up?"

"Wonderful, that's it. Now turn to the camera. Miss Tina, I'm gonna make you a star."

"How about just making me rich?" I tease.

"Okay, I'll buy you a Mercedes."

"Martin, you've got a deal."

"Beverly, get that pencil out of your mouth and look into my camera. That's it, that's it."

Eva giggles and rushes over to Martin to smell whatever it is he's talking about. She's never seen an invisible camera before. It doesn't smell any different than Martin's fingers. Martin focuses on the door, the film advances, and Ricardo lumbers in on cue.

"And presenting the Ricardo," Martin announces.

Ricardo looks around the room in wonder and ignores his brief encounter with fame.

"How do you like the way the room is shaping up, Ricardo?" Kaye asks, staple gun in hand.

"When I looked inside, I thought I was dreaming." He smiles shyly and my heart flutters. Yes, he's softening; he's changing ever so slightly, but significantly enough for us to notice. I'm proud of him.

"Finish your work and then you can help me hang up pictures. How does that sound?"

"Good." He smiles at her. Kaye's offer takes Ricardo through his math paper with only a few grimaces and quiet rumblings. But by the time he begins his handwriting, hope scatters like tumbleweed.

"I can't do this dumb thing. I can't do it! Do you hear me? Are ya deaf or somethin'? I can't do it!"

Paper and hope are rolled up in a ball and thrown in Martin's direction. Ricardo storms to the door with his hand gripping the doorknob but miraculously, he doesn't turn it. He just stands there poised for action, stewing and steaming but stays inside the classroom. Kaye and I ignore him and don't even ask him to return to his seat. Since he hasn't been challenged or reprimanded, he releases the doorknob and quietly slides into his seat again. He can save face, yet he's still a victim of his own outbursts. They no longer feel good; if they ever served him, he can't remember how. Ricardo hides his face in his arms so no one sees the tears.

> *'Hello, hello, hello,' he calls to the high cliffs.*
> *'Hello, hello, hello,' they answer. 'Do you hear*
> *me, hear me, hear me?' His voice cries into the*
> *shrieking darkness. 'Hear me, hear me, hear me,'*
> *the mountains echo.*

When I get home, I realize that tomorrow is Valentine's Day. I'm not one to go in for chocolates and flowers and soft animal toys with 'I love you' banners around their fluffy necks. In many ways, I feel this festival is nothing more than a corporate sham. Still, despite myself, I stifle the smallest little shadow of disappointment that creeps into my mind while making my dinner: 'You'll be alone on Valentine's!' I push the voice away—I'm happy with my life, pursuing my dreams and my goals. I'm not compromising my ideals and I'm living what I truly believe.

February 14

I wake up this morning after a weird dream that disturbs me. In the dream I come into school carrying my pumping heart in my hands.

"Let's see it!" they scream, and push one another.

"It's mine, it's mine!" Ricardo yells, punching Beverly.

"I wants it. I wants it." Beverly tries to sneak it away from me.

"I must have it. I will have it," Martin warns us all.

"It's for Eva, a present for Eva."

They pull at my heart till it shreds and each of them grabs a handful.

"It's not beating anymore," Ricardo complains, and chucks his piece in the wastebasket.

The dream stays with me throughout my shower and bathroom routine and well into breakfast. I grab a coffee in my travel mug and jump in the car, my heart still reeling from its nocturnal assault. Is that what I really feel? Do my students drain me so much? I'll admit sometimes I feel emotionally and physically exhausted after remaining calm despite their flare-ups, insults and backslides. I've never felt defeated, just weary, but always ready to resume the challenge after a good rest or friendly company.

Maybe the dream's only warning me to keep some of my heart left over for me and the others in my life that count. Advice well taken! I have to call Mom. She sent me a Valentine's card like always. How does she do it, anyway? How does she find time to care for us so? I clear my head and listen to calming music on the way into work, one hand on the wheel, the other clasped tightly around my coffee cup.

Martin's been trying to find a mailman's uniform all week. He tells me he would have stolen a mail truck but he believes in non-violence and can't drive. Instead, he's settled for a sailor's cap and a laundry bag his mother's given him on the promise that he would tell Donald Duck and Peter Rabbit that they'll have to find other living quarters and make different arrangements for their meals.

"My mother said there aren't enough chairs at the table, Miss Tina. She's going to give my portion away to the others. And there are four of us. She's going to divide my breakfast, lunch and dinner into four. How can she do that? I'll be hungry forever and ever and what will happen to me?"

"Why into four, Martin?" I ask, excited that Martin is revealing more about his vivid, imaginary life.

"That's simple, Miss Tina. Mister X always dines at home. And up till now Donald and Peter ate with us too. I agreed about the Duck and the Rabbit only because it's Valentine's Day and I didn't want to break my mother's heart. But this is too hard to take," he sniffles. "I told Peter I'll go on a hunger strike to protest, but I can't on Valentine's Day. I just can't; not when I need to transport all these valentine cards to school. And I don't want to upset my mother. Not today!"

"Martin, I'm sure you and your mother will work this out. Maybe you can find good homes for Peter and Donald. Maybe they'll be just as happy and there will be a lot more food for you and Mister X to share so you won't starve."

Martin pauses and considers my comments. He grins and nods at me. "You may be right, Miss Tina. You are smart and I have just the card for you."

"Thank you, Martin, you're very kind." He extends the purple envelope to me with a bow.

"Miss Kaye, I have something you're gonna love!"

"Really, Martin, I wonder what that could be? Is it something to eat?"

"No, it's better!"

King Zagoot is impatient. He's signaled his royal treasurer for days now and all he gets is static. He's planning to surprise the new earth ladies in his life with a necklace of precious jewels from the next galaxy but first he has to buy them. And there's no foreign exchange for Zagootian currency on earth, although he's looking into that.

Lately business is consuming most of his time and Planet Zagoot is not cooperating with him at all. The last contact he had confirmed an uprising. It seems that in his absence, the royal family, led by his ruthless sister, attempted to seize the throne from him. The townsfolk angrily stampeded the palace to protest the takeover. The family is now imprisoned. Thanks to his devoted subjects, he's still supreme.

However, the royal cook has fled to save his own life, and his wife remains, poking her nose in the gooseberry pie. Now things will never be the same.

"I can't guess. What is it, Martin?"

"Do you give up?"

"Yes, yes."

"Here. It's a Valentine's Day card for you."

"Thank you, Martin. That's very thoughtful of you."

Everyone receives a card from Martin. We paint big red hearts to take home and somehow Beverly manages to streak the floor red despite the layers of newspaper. Eva makes two hearts.

"One for Grandma," Eva explains. "I'm going to Grandma's house."

Before Ricardo leaves, he walks up to me with his hands behind him.

"Here, this is for you," he stammers. He pulls out a still wet heart and hands it to me.

"Thanks, Ricardo, I love it!"

My dream rushes back to me and I smile. This new heart is bigger than the discarded original. And look how many more life years it has.

February 23

"I'm leaving school," Martin threatens me. Everyone has earned playtime, that is, everyone but Martin. Absorbed in ethereal matters, he neglects his mundane responsibility to the world of mathematics. He has printed his name on the 8 ½ x 11 inch sheet, so I know he's aware of its existence. That's all I know. Lunch time is approaching. Martin knows that without his work papers completed, there's not much happening for him on the culinary plane. Mister X is not very pleased. He likes his meals on schedule.

"Goodbye, Martin," I call to him as he's lowering the rubber dinghy down from the port side of the boat.

"I won't be back anymore."

"I'm sorry to hear that, Martin. I'll miss you, but if you won't be back here anymore, well, then you won't be back."

"Yeah," Martin assents, trudging to the closet where the life jackets and life preservers are kept.

"You know, I guess we'll have to find another child to take your place. Later on today I'll ask Mr. Strong if he knows another boy who would like to be in this class."

"Who?"

"Oh, I don't know. I'll ask if we can have a boy who behaves well and finishes all his work. I'm sure he can find someone who wants to be with us."

"Well, maybe I'll leave after I have my lunch. Mister X doesn't want me to leave anyway. He likes it here. And he got 100 percent on his spelling paper. He knows he needs me around though. Come on, Mister X, tie up my life jacket and we can go to our last lunch together."

"That's a good idea, Martin. Then you won't be hungry for your long walk home. We'd like to have you stay and eat lunch with us on your last day."

Martin resumes his position at the helm and with the help of Miss Kaye and Mister X he performs his navigational maneuvers easily. Lunch is eaten; we have our current events, story-time and music activities. The dinghy remains secured to the boat and no one mentions Martin's projected desertion, not even Martin.

March 2

Eva lies down on the cot we have in the play area. Talking to herself, she ritualizes the words.

"I get up in the morning." She gets up. "I brush my teeth. I wash my hands."

> *She remembers to install a bedroom and a bathroom in the house. The bedroom is furnished in walnut so it will be strong and unbending.*
>
> *She sews angel hair into the pillow for softness and lays down a lavender goose-feather quilt to nestle under when she's cold. The plants on the windowsill she waters and talks to every day to make them grow faster.*

"Hi, Miss Tina. Hi, Eva. Hi, Miss Kaye," Beverly greets us.

"Hi," Eva says, not looking away from the scrambled eggs she's cooking on the stove.

We have a morning pantomime. Beverly is a bird, Ricardo's the fiercest tiger, overturning chairs and scaring Eva, who only wants to eat her breakfast, write words and go to sleep—in that order. Martin decides to be a toaster and burns all the toast till he runs to the store himself to buy another loaf of bread. No one guesses what he is and Ricardo angrily leaves the circle. With hands held high above his sweaty body, the victorious wrestler outwits his opponents once again.

"I won, I won." Martin bows to the cheering crowd.

"That's 'cause you cheated. You always cheat. You're a cheater and a baby and I wish you'd get lost."

"Oh yeah?"

"Yeah, you little punk." Ricardo taunts.

"Oh yeah?"

"Cut it out or I'll mess you up. I'll kill you if ya don't stop, ya hear me?"

Martin believes he's invincible and one 'oh yeah' too many slips from his mouth. Ricardo tackles him. I pry them apart.

"Get your filthy hands off me." Ricardo attempts to bite my arm. "Go away from me, you bitch. Keep your hands off me." He kicks and writhes as I hold him.

"I told you I'm not going to let you hurt anyone in here. I'm not going to let you hurt yourself, either. I'm stronger than you are. When you're able to control yourself and calm down, I'll let you go."

Ricardo kicks till he is war-weary and convinced that I really can harness the unbridled rage. He stops kicking and biting me and I release him.

> *He is caged in by the fury and the terror. They are his prison wardens. In the morning the fury slams into him, and he wakens. He is held down for his breakfast, they feed him injections of iodized salt to soak up the tears like atomic sponges.*
>
> *Night is when terror seizes him and squeezes out whatever is left of his dried-up rage. Do his insides dehydrate and die when everything is emptied out of them? Then what is it like to be alone with himself in a cell without windows?*

"Ricardo," Kaye walks in the room and immediately comes to his rescue and mine. "I need someone strong to help me with these books before they fall."

He is by her side, unloading some of the bundle from her arms. Luckily, Martin, his buddy and competitor, is too busy with his spelling words to care.

March 10

"I went to play yesterday," Bev divulges. "They don't call me ugly no more. They don't call me stinky no more. The kids is outside playin'. My mommy says the kids want to play with me. Bring my big wheels out. Girls ride big wheels?"

"Yes, Beverly. Girls ride big wheels like you do."

"Girls ride bicycles?"

"And bicycles."

> *Inside the mirror she finds a splintered smile,*
> *she plucks it till it's smooth and fits easily within the*
> *rest of her face. With the wood splinters she mends*
> *a music box and bends her ear to listen to the song*
> *inside.*

"A funky comedy called *Which Way is Up*, rated R, that's what I'm going to see," Martin tells us.

It isn't reviewed yet; it hasn't been viewed yet. He and Mister X are invited to a private screening at Chez Bernard—an exclusive club for invisibles and those who are neither here nor there. Martin finds group cohesion so provincial; he doesn't align himself with any organization. He got just where he is by his own enterprising individualism. Anyway, he's never alone. If Mister X isn't with him, there's always Donald Duck or Martin Mouse.

Now that he's found both of them and Peter Rabbit good homes, he occasionally brings them to school so he can visit with them. His mother made it real clear they aren't to return to the Selby house. No, never again in this lifetime. King Zagoot stops in to visit, too. Martin's never lacking in friends. They always come around just to see if he's there and find out what he's up to. He hasn't time to think about being alone. His friends wouldn't allow him to worry about it.

Mister X vouches for Martin and they are escorted to a table in the front of the restaurant near the stage. Martin spies King Zagoot, who is posing as a foreign agent.

King Zagoot is exposed and arrested by scouts of the royal family. They give him a dime to make one last call.

When he puts the dime in the nowhere telephone to contact Zagoot, an operator insists on repeating to him in clothespin drawl: 'I'm sorry, but the number you have reached is not in service in this area code.'

King Zagoot tosses the dime to Martin. "Keep trying," he whispers encouragingly, as they handcuff him.

"Hi, Martin," Eva sniffs his black wool cape. "How do you spell your name?"

"M-a-r-t-i-n. What a girl. You know how to spell it, you are a wonder woman!" Martin flips the cape in a sweeping gesture across his shoulder. Only then do I notice a black patch across his left eye.

"Martin, what happened to your eye?"

"Ssshhh, I'm an enemy spy," he whispers and investigates under the desks and in the closet.

"What are you looking for? I might be able to help you."

"A clue."

"A clue for what?"

"To find out where they've taken him."

"Who have they taken and who are they?" I'm more confused than when I began.

"It's a secret, a top secret fit for a king. Sshh, they might hear you."

"Who might hear me?" I'm whispering, playing along. More sharing of his internal espionage and I want to make sure he feels he can openly confide in me.

"They've taken the king. That's all I can tell you now. Sshh, someone's coming. All right, now turn around and walk in slow and easy. I don't want to hurt you."

Ricardo inches into the room backwards and then leaps onto Martin.

"Now get up before I whip you. Come on, get up," dares Ricardo.

"Okay, Ricardo and Martin, I need someone to give out the breakfasts. Martin, let's have you do that. Ricardo, will you help me set up the film projector?"

"Yeah."

"And Martin?"

"Yes, Miss Tina?"

"We have exactly four cereals today. I'm sorry."

Martin and Mister X agree to flip a coin. Mister X has only Swiss bills and Martin spent this week's allowance on disguises so he doesn't have any spare change. He knows Mister X has some revealing information about the king's whereabouts, quite possibly a lead. So he lets Mister X have the chocolate milk and the Kellogg's Frosted Flakes. It's not every day a king is abducted.

During the film about animals, Martin positions his chair between both girls and protectively puts his arms around them. Beverly laughs and Eva has him autograph her notebook. Ricardo sits away from the fan club and delivers cat calls as the giraffe wiggles into view.

March 12

Martin's real quiet. His hunger strike failed and his mother has impolitely kicked out all his friends. Mister X embarks on a special assignment of espionage.

"Martin, how about finishing your work on time today?" Kaye asks him. Martin bursts into tears.

"I can't do it by myself, Miss Kaye."

"Okay, come up to my desk and I'll help you."

Martin sits by Kaye's desk throughout the morning. With all his companions gone, he asks if he can share his lunch with her. Kaye agrees and Martin tearfully hands Kaye half of his bologna sandwich.

Beverly approaches me, pulling at the sleeve of her right arm with her left hand.

"You know what I want, Miss Tina? I want bubbles, you know. They fly."

"Soap bubbles. You want soap bubbles. Birds fly, planes fly, and soap bubbles fly. Beverly wants to fly."

"Les."

We make cardboard replicas of our bodies. Beverly's has two arms sticking out of the stomach.

"Beverly, look where your arms are. See," I point in the mirror as I touch her, "they are attached to your shoulders."

Eva takes the glue and makes black curls down the doll's head with pieces of yarn she cuts. Ricardo colors in a black patch over one eye and three black teeth.

"Miss Kaye, look at my man," Ricardo brings the cardboard boy up to her desk.

"Ricardo, I think that's wonderful. It's great. Do you mean to tell me that you did it all by yourself?"

He nods. "Well, I am real proud of you."

Martin takes a long time to decide what his should look like. He cuts out a beret from black construction paper and plasters down a felt goatee and moustache to the face.

"Who that?" Beverly inquires.

"Bernard," Martin introduces us. When no one is looking, Martin sticks pins into Ricardo's doll. Nothing happens.

"I won't be here tomorrow. I is goin' to the hospital."

"Why do you have to go to the hospital tomorrow?"

"I hurt."

"Where do you hurt, Bev?"

"Here," she taps her stomach. Martin is puzzled. He looks at the table again just to make sure the pins are on the right body. He's certain he pricked Ricardo's cardboard belly with the pointed needles.

March 13

Eva writes 'Beverly' on the blackboard.
"Where's Beverly?"
"She's in the hospital, Eva."
"How do you spell hospital?" Eva prints the word alongside Beverly's name.

> *Her mother waves goodbye and they wheel Bev*
> *inside and lock the doors behind them. Everything*
> *is white. The masks over their faces glow white,*
> *and the wafer they give her to melt on her tongue is*
> *white.*
> *They slice down the middle and find a pitchfork*
> *there in her belly. One of them dislodges it with big*
> *tweezers and slides it under her pillow till morning*
> *when she finds it.*
> *When her mother comes to take her back home,*
> *she offers her mother the pitchfork to lean on like*
> *a crutch, while she leaps over the cracks in the*
> *sidewalk.*

March 24

"Welcome back, Beverly. We missed you."
"Hi, I ain't got no 'ernia no more. I don't hurt. See," Beverly lifts up her shirt and displays her fresh scar.
"For Beverly." Eva sniffs the scar and gives Beverly the get well card we drew for her.
"Does it hurt?"
"Not no more. It ficked up now."

Eva looks at her own bellybutton but there are no salient markings there.

"My mommy yelled at me. My mommy scared me," Eva confides in lieu of a seam on her stomach. Martin screeches up in his ambulance and medic uniform and sticks a thermometer in Beverly's mouth.

"Now, this won't hurt. Say 'ah'."

"Ah."

"Oh no! This could be real serious! You're boiling up, girl. You are hot, hot, hot and soon you're going to BOOM all over the place. Better lie down."

Their play unfolds a short distance from my desk. Fascinated, I watch as their worlds converge and their fantasies are shared in play. Martin steeps the herbal brew, borrowed from the ancient wisdom of the alchemists and Zagootian home remedies. Now that King Zagoot is missing, he can't remember the Zagootian formula to counteract loneliness. Eva stands over Martin to ensure precision and because the aromatic vapors of myrrh and bayberry are irresistible. The concoction is presented to Beverly by Zaspirilla: Martin's newest companion, royal magician and ventriloquist. To the disfavor of everyone, Beverly sputters and ambrosia flies everywhere.

"Okay, ladies and gentlemen, don't come any closer. Stand back, this is dangerous. We will have to operate." He gouges a hole with a rubber surgical knife and cayenne speckles spill out of Beverly's stomach onto the stretcher. "I think you'll make it." A white sheet is thrown over Beverly's head just in case she is really dead.

In the afternoon, Martin and Ricardo choose the horseshoes. Martin is losing.

"My brother will drill holes in your head. My mother's going to beat you with her egg beater."

"I'm gonna pick up your mother's dress in front of you." Ricardo counters.

"Oh, what he said," Martin giggles while his cousin-twice-removed clucks disapprovingly.

"Martin and Ricardo, this is between you two and not between anyone's brother and mother. Martin, your mother's not angry with Ricardo, you're angry because he's winning. It's important to take responsibility for how you feel and not blame anyone else for your feelings."

The game ends when Ricardo bombards Martin and Beverly with horseshoes.

March 26

Greetings, Earthlings!

"Who has news today? Is there something you want to share with us, Martin?" It's difficult not to notice Martin's hand, like a conductor's baton flashing in front of me.

"I'm mad." His mouth is upturned into the angriest smile I've ever seen.

"Aw, he was mad yesterday. You put that up on the board yesterday. He's such a little copycat."

"Sometimes a person is angry two days in a row, Ricardo. It's all right if Martin feels angry again today."

"What are you mad about, Martin?" Kaye inquires.

"I'm mad because I'm mad," our existentialist retorts.

> *Mister X discovers where they're holding King Zagoot captive. The Zagootian citizens send an envoy to the tower but when the earthlings spot a Zagootian spaceship they fire on it, forcing it down. Unharmed, the twice captured king is now an earth prisoner.*
>
> *The royal cook is also taken, his silverware confiscated, and the Zagootian spaceship is detained for observation. Mister X is bored with third rate hotels and philistine nationalists calling him comrade. He wishes to return but there's a misunder-*

standing concerning his expense account. The bank regretfully reports to him that he is conspicuously overdrawn.

March 27

"Say torpedo."
"Torpedo."
"Say missile."
"Missile."
"Say grenade."
"Grenade."

Chasing Eva around the room in paratrooper fashion, Martin instructs her in the art of verbal warfare while he grooms himself for hand-to-hand combat. As for Eva, she familiarizes herself with war lingo because someday she's going to be a nurse on the front line. Eva's fingers have engaged Martin as her mentor until future notice.

You Can't Make an Omelet
without Breaking a Few Eggs

March 28

I dream I hear someone calling my name over and over again in a thin faraway voice. "Where are you?" I murmur, stroking the opaque curtain of darkness. The curtain yawns open; a shivering egg rolls into my hand. I carry the egg asleep in my glove and surprise eight watchful eyes.

My night-dreams are intensifying lately. I drive to school while trying to make sense out of last night's dream. There's something to attend to here, some meaning to my dreams. Frequent dreaming of my students may be a sign of the need for a mini vacation and some time with friends. I could enjoy a good dinner party and a few days walking in the woods. Easter's more than two weeks away, so I'd better be patient and get on with my professional life. I arrive at school to a little surprise.

"Look, Tina, it's an emergency placement. This is the only suitable class for the child. He won't really fit anywhere else. Mother and child will pop in this afternoon to meet you," says the guidance counselor.

"But so near the end of the school year. We're just beginning to function as a group. What's going to happen now?"

"You'll manage, you always do." Mr. Strong hands me the file, pats my shoulder encouragingly and walks out of the office.

"Thanks. Warn me, please." How's that for a dream that has some semblance of my reality? Maybe the 'shivering egg' in my dream is Warren, the new student to arrive. Wow! I wonder how I could've known that in advance. As I await my students' arrival, with the new 'profile' under my arm, I feel a little put-upon, but sure that I can rise to the challenge. I always knew that, in this job, you have to be flexible! This is just one of those times.

Eva comes in with a new doll.

"Look what Grandma bought me, Miss Tina."

"Your grandma is very good to you. It's a beautiful doll."

"What that?" Beverly wants to see.

"Eva's doll. Eva's grandma gave her a doll."

"Eva, want to sit wit me?" Beverly asks casually.

"No!" There's no uncertainty in her response.

"It's time for our morning story, everyone. Bring your chairs up to the front."

Eva screams, "No, I don't want to work. I want to play."

"Eva, you can play after our work. We have to stop now."

"Nooooo!"

"Who wants to do that stinky work anyway? You always make us work. That's all we ever do in this damn place. I shoulda stayed home." Count on Ricardo to be another voice of dissent.

"Well, Ricardo, you didn't stay at home. You are in school and here we work and play."

"I want to work. I got a new phonics book and I'm gonna finish it and do all the pages. Right, Miss Kaye?"

"I hope so, Martin."

"Why did he get a new book? Why didn't I get a new book? You're not fair. You just give him a book."

"Ricardo, when you're ready you can have a new book, too."

"Yeah, I get to read all those dumb baby words. How come he don't have to read those stupid words?"

"When you can read the words in Martin's book, you can have a book like his."

"Oh yeah, I can read 'em. Gimme a book. I'll show ya I ain't no dummy. I can read as good as him."

"Okay, Ricardo, if you're able to read the words in Martin's book, you may have one."

Ricardo left his rabbit's foot at home, and he's never believed in miracles. He reads falteringly. There are too many words on the page and only a handful of recognizable ones. The book misses the waste paper basket by a hair.

"I don't want it, anyway. You can keep your old crappy books. I don't care. Why should I care?"

> *He calls to all the squirrels in the park. 'Come here, look what I have for you.' Down from the branches they scurry and gather around him. See, I brought you some nuts.'*
> *'These are not nuts!' a squirrel in back shouts. 'Can't you read the label? These are cracker-jacks. We don't like crackerjacks!'*
> *They race away into the oak trees and shake acorns down on his weary head.*

"Eva, why don't you bring your new doll up here and tell us about it?"

Beverly, Eva, and Martin come into the circle.

"Today I have news for all of us. Do you remember when you first came into this class?"

"I remember." It's a wonder Martin remembers anything with the superabundance of information he's stored. Martin can tell you what he had for an evening snack two weeks ago, what you wore to his sister's high school graduation, and direct you to his house from almost any point in the city, citing landmarks, lights, and winding turns. With the same ease, Martin will recite all the places Mister X has visited in the last three years and probably be able to supply you with information regarding your family tree. He never forgets his; they follow him everywhere. One of his vintage great-great-aunts returned a fortnight ago to chastise Martin for the late hours he's keeping. It seems Martin has, along with the scarlet fever, a history of insomnia. Would you be able to sleep if your head were a ham radio and other operators clamored to be on your frequency?

The family physicians, Uncle Zeke and Cousin Otis, have prescribed medication for Martin's 'condition' but with minimal success. Mister X doesn't see any change in Martin, not one that's more favorable. Since Mister X's return, he's closely observed Martin and finds him more mercenary and intolerable than before and now Martin's temper is flaring up. Mister X is surreptitiously scouting around for a new employer. Send all applications and references to Post Office Box 000 and please don't forget to enclose a family snapshot.

What about Eva? Eva's recollection is prenatal. She recalls sloshing and slapping uneasily against uterine walls and sounds of piped-in human breathing. The fragrance of her womb-chamber is still with her.

After Beverly's operation, her memory was restored. She's now convinced of a direct relationship between her stomach and her brain.

"Some time after lunch today, another boy is going to come into our class and be with us."

"Who's comin'?" Ricardo's survival button is pushed by the phrase 'another boy.'

"His name is Warren and he's seven years old."

"A baby class. That's what this joint is turning into. A bunch of pissy, smelly, damned babies." Ricardo's disgust is visible all over his frowning face.

"Yeah, pissy babies who go around the room crying, "Waaaaaa, waaaaa!"

Martin thinks 'pissy' has such a lyrical quality to it.

"Well, he better not do somethin' I don't like 'cause I'll kill him."

"It seems that you're going to kill a lot of people if they don't do what you want, Ricardo."

"Yeah, I'll kill 'em all right. I ain't no baby."

"If he messes with me, I'll turn him into pantyhose!" Martin adds. Martin and Ricardo laugh lustily.

"I don't know anything more about him. I'd like you to be nice to him and let him get to know us and our classroom. You all remember how it felt when you first arrived here and you didn't know anybody. You felt shy and felt like you had to protect yourselves."

"He's gonna have to learn the rules," Ricardo grins.

"Yes, we all have to work within the rules Ricardo, that's right. And one of the rules is to be nice to each other. So let's all remember that when he's here."

The morning is forever. If there was any semblance of group cohesion, it's now extinct. Eva doesn't want to work and Beverly is in a comatose state. Ricardo and Martin can't focus on anything that is not nylon and linked to feminine undergarments. They snigger and giggle and tell nonsensical 'jokes' to verbalize this titillating vocabulary with each other.

My solution is to hand out headphones and plug them into the world of audio. Not only does this lesson develop listening skills but it wards off migraine headaches and teacher burnout. In the middle of our second chorus of the sing-a-long cassette tape, the door opens and three people eye us strangely. The earth people have gone Martian. Martin noiselessly conducts a soundless orchestra while the rest of us have wire rising out of our heads connecting us to the mother electrical circuit.

"Good Morning, Miss Tina. This is Warren."

The school counselor beams at me a little distractedly. He seems eager to leave and get back to other more pressing responsibilities. I know he cares; he's been my greatest supporter at the school. He knows more than the other teachers how challenging these kids can be. I've watched him firsthand with parents and with my kids, especially Eva, and he's a pro.

As Mr. Strong takes his leave, ushering Mom down the corridor to handle the remaining formalities, Warren flops himself on the floor, cries and pounds his head with his fists. He's one of the tiniest children I've ever seen, with long mouse-shaped ears and an angular chin. As I bend down to stop him, I inhale the heavy scent of his mother's perfume. He won't stop and bangs his head hard against the floor; his fists clench.

"Warren, let's stop hurting ourselves." I hold his hands in mine. Tears trickle down his small face and he sobs without noise. He squirms out of my arms and hides himself under a desk. There he stays till his mother returns from her discussion with the school counselor.

"He's a little shy," Mrs. Jackson explains. "He'll get used to you. When he does, he won't hide all the time."

"How does Warren communicate? Does he talk to you?"

"Well, he repeats what I say sometimes," she sighs, "but Warren doesn't talk much at all."

Warren holds onto his mother's hand and punches his chest as they walk out.

"Mrs. Jackson, let's arrange to talk together. I want to learn more about Warren."

"Yes, that's fine. I really hope Warren adjusts here. He never adjusted at the last school." Mrs. Jackson's voice lowers. "Warren spent more time at home with me. Frankly, I don't believe they knew how to handle Warren's behavior."

"Goodbye, Warren," I call.

"Boy, he's cuckoo." Ricardo's subdued. "Did ya see him hit himself?"

"Yeah," Martin agrees.

What is it Eva is remembering with her fingers?

Zaspirilla offers to entertain us with a magic show, but we decline. No one wants to talk and their work is completed without incident. Apprehension enshrouds us like a thick fog.

"Is he gonna be back here tomorrow?" Ricardo asks on his way out the door.

"Yes," I smile, "we'll all be here."

"That kid could hurt himself doin' like he was doin.' "

"You know something, Ricardo, you're absolutely right. See you tomorrow."

March 30

"Martin, what on earth are you laughing at?"
"The rabbit in the radiator."
Well, that explains it. "Now I see it."
"Not everybody can see him. He's invisible."
"I see him," Ricardo grins. "Look, he's winking."
"His name is Peter," Martin volunteers.

> *A special bulletin is released on planet Zagoot. The royal cook is now the official head chef of the earth prison where King Zagoot is interned. The King is in good health, unharmed, and relishes every delectable meal. When he eats, his homesickness subsides. The royal cook insists that the King get unlimited helpings of anything he wants.*
>
> *Consequently, the King's royal pants need alteration. The King requests that his royal tailor zagoot down immediately and furnish him with new garments. The King is hopeful and proselytizes to his cellmates.*
>
> *'More heaven than hell' is taking hold among the earth prisoners. Already there are ten converts.*
>
> *One of them is the warden who's consented to hang up plaques with the new logo. Banners that proclaim 'more heaven than hell' are everywhere throughout the prison, even in rooms designated 'employees only'.*
>
> *The warden covertly circulates the Zagootian doctrine on the outside. When the King is freed, he promises to zagoot the warden to his planet to see*

*the meteorite races and the Miss Galaxy contest,
which coincidentally will be held on Zagoot this
year. The warden procures an entry blank for his
sister.*

Warren's seat is underneath his desk. He comes out to go to the bathroom, for his lunch and to go home. I don't know why he bothers to surface for lunch; he doesn't eat any. With his fingers like pincers, he picks up a fraction of a French fry, smells it, closes his eyes and tastes it. Two fries a day are his quota. He stares at the peas and pushes them around with his fork. He won't touch them. Yesterday he did the same thing with his carrots. Jell-O, he's decided, is amoeba. Everything is alive for him. Only white bread and French fries are dead. When he eats them, nothing catastrophic happens.

Kaye hangs a clothesline for the dolls' clothes. Beverly and Eva wash the clothes in the sink, and Eva explains to herself as she works, "I wash the clothes. I put them on the line. They smell fresh. They smell clean." She sniffs them admiringly, pleased with her handiwork. Beverly hangs her doll's clothes alongside Eva's on the line.

"It smells good."

*They open their purses and hand the cashier
their money. They push through the turnstile and
rush past the main gate of the amusement park.
Beverly buys peanuts and Eva shows her how to
shell them.*

*On the roller coaster they hold hands and
squeal as it careens downward. Eva slaps a quarter
down on number seven, the roulette wheel spins and
number seven wins. Eva selects a doll as her prize.*

*Beverly's angry. She buys a strawberry double-
dipped ice cream cone and won't give Eva a lick.*

"That's my mommy," Eva announces when her mother comes in to talk with me.

Mrs. Turner is excited about Eva's progress. Now Eva talks to her and asks questions all the time. Eva can do more for herself and the tantrums have subsided. As Mrs. Turner is leaving though, Eva wants to leave with her mother and resorts to the old crying, screaming fits.

At this, Warren huddles against the desk leg. Loud noises terrify him. His world is comprised of hushed whispers and icy tears. When he flogs himself he knows he's still here. He pulls at his genitals and slams his head against the floor to tell us he wishes he weren't here at all. He appears as if the world were crawling around inside his flesh like parasites that suck his blood and multiply instantly. Maybe he will destroy himself first, before they finish him.

"I want to go home!" Eva shouts.

"You can't come home now, Sweetie. I'll see you when the bus drops you off."

"I want to go, Mommy. I want to go," she yells after her mother.

"Eva, you'll see your mommy later. Would you like to come up here with me and write a story together?"

Eva has a proclivity for words. She is awed by the results they produce and the ever-present fact that when she opens her mouth words mysteriously rush out.

Eva writes her story slanting down the right side of the paper. Proudly she reads. "A monster is biting some people. They are scared. They're going to run to their mother. Then they'll go to bed."

"Is Eva scared?"

"Eva scared. I went to Brigantine Castle. The monsters scared me."

"They're not real monsters. They are pretend ones."

"Not real?"

"No, not real."

If words are real and monster is a word, then how can monsters not be real? Eva is puzzled. "Monsters are not real." Eva and her fingers discuss this illusive quality.

"Oh, yes, they are. They are really, really real! They chase you around the room and when they get you, they throw you in jail." Martin runs after Eva with an amorphous bow. Arrows dipped in Zaspirilla's special love oil shoot into Eva's heart. Eva giggles and flings the arrows at Ricardo, who catches them, breaks them in two, and gently rolls one to Warren. Beverly screams.

"Beverly, why did you yell?" I ask.

"I want to."

April 1

Mister X announces a change in his mailing address. It seems that someone is snooping around in his belongings. A letter with the King's insignia seal was steamed open. Send all correspondence to his Aunt Flora in London. She knows how to keep a secret.

> *The prison affairs committee convenes and decides that retaining a Zagootian king on earth is costly. Overhead has almost tripled since his incarceration.*
>
> *Food consumption has increased. The prisoners now want a lounge with a skylight erected in the north wing, and a telescope. They demand one full hour of stargazing in the evening right before bed.*
>
> *Refreshments are to be served in the lounge area by Zagootian waitresses and curfew is to be extended until sunrise. One of the petitions seized insists on a sauna and heart-shaped indoor swimming pool.*
>
> *In adjourning, the committee members resolve to permit the King access to any escape hatch he likes as quickly as possible.*

Martin wears his thermal spacesuit to school. "I'm going to blast off into space in my rocket ship and I will be gone forever."

"But Martin," Kaye argues, "if you do we may never see you again."

Kaye's right. Things would be pretty colorless around here without Martin.

"Well, maybe I'll zoom down and visit, but I must go. I must. There's no other way."

Ricardo wants Martin to bequeath his goggles to him. Eva wants his beret and splashy yellow slicker with the wet look. As for Beverly, she'll take anything Martin's leaving behind. I request his video camera and Kaye chooses his sheepskin coat. We are all pleased with the arrangements. All but Martin. He didn't know leaving everything behind would be such a hardship. Martin cries and throws his Spiderman lunchbox across the floor.

"We have to go, Miss Kaye," Martin sobs. "We just have to."

"Martin, it's a pity you have to leave before our Easter party. Do you think you might be able to stay around just for that, and then you could leave?"

Did someone say Easter party? Mister X graciously accepts the invitation. Of course he will attend the fete. He's rather enervated from his previous airborne escapades and dizzy charades. No one is going to compel him to leave terra firma. Not even Martin.

"I guess I could stay for the party, Miss Tina. I will arrange it."

The spacesuit is hung in the closet next to Martin's army fatigues, and a worn-out saddle which belonged to Ricardo's charger. Martin walks downstairs with Kaye to get the lunches.

"Okay, Beverly, let's try to write your name again. The B is turned the wrong way. See, this is the way it faces."

Eva rushes over to Ricardo's desk, gets close enough to sniff his face, murmurs his name and then hops back to her own seat.

"Aw, leave me alone. Get your face outta here."

"Ricardo, Ricardo. How do you spell your name?" asks Eva.

He doesn't answer. Warren emerges from his hidcout to go to the bathroom.

"Let me take him, Miss Tina. I can take him."

I'm stunned by Ricardo's request. Is something akin to compassion and brotherly concern taking hold in him? Whatever it is, I can't ignore the sincerity behind his question and how much it reflects his growth. I take in a deep breath before I speak. Hesitantly, I agree and watch as Ricardo gently holds Warren's hand and carefully leads him across the hall to the bathroom with Kaye shadowing them the whole time. They return unharmed and Ricardo confides in me.

"You know, he can't even open the door. I hadda do it for him."

"Thanks, Ricardo, you really are a good helper."

"Ladies and gentlemen, the chicken dog man is here and lunch is now served." Martin has recovered from his upset and peace reigns for our noontime meal.

It's so rare these days that Kaye and I have a chance to talk together. We usually wait until the day's end when everyone is safely on their bus to grab a few moments to sum up what's been happening with the children and strategize what comes next. Today is no different. After seeing the last child off, Kaye reenters the classroom and flops in a chair.

"You know Tina, I never imagined that this job would be like this: exhaustion right down to my feet." She sighs.

"You're right. It takes its toll. Do you regret being assigned to this class, Kaye?"

"At first I was annoyed, you know that. I didn't think they were paying me enough to do this job. And they're not. But now, these kids have grown on me. It's amazing how much I care for them."

"I probably don't tell you enough how much you help me and how much I appreciate you."

"Yeah, you do, but thanks anyway. I like hearing the praise." Kaye grins in her teasing way, part serious, part playful. It's amazing how well we fit together.

"What happened with you and Ricardo earlier?"

"He was so angry and upset with himself for losing it. Tina, he's really trying. He just can't help it."

"I know but he's getting better. The outbursts aren't as often or as violent as before. Look what he did for Warren. That kind act brought tears to my eyes."

"Me too. But I like Ricardo's spunk, you know," Kaye murmurs softly.

"I don't want him to lose that, Kaye. It's so him. I just want Ricardo to have more self-control, less anger and more internal resources. And feel good about who he is with good strategies at his disposal."

"That's all?" Kaye looks at me, grinning and we both laugh.

"Maybe that's a tall order but I believe he's up to it. Excelling in reading would be a plus, too. Do you remember when he first came here and refused to work at all?"

"I remember. You've worked miracles, Tina."

"Miracles, thanks, but I don't know that they're really miracles. I believe it's my job."

"Believe me, you've done wonders."

"Only with your help," I smile at Kaye as we ready each student's work folder for the next day.

"Pour it on, please. Pour it on." Kaye pretends to splash the praise like body mist all over. We both laugh. Did I forget to mention that one of the prerequisites for this job was an intact and lively sense of humor? Another prerequisite is a vivid imagination.

April 3

"Who can tell me what animal this is?"

"A horse." Eva's discerning nose recognizes the scent even from a picture.

"That's right. Where do horses live?"

"In a horse factory so all the people in television land live on horse meat," laughs Martin.

"You're such a little liar, there ain't no such thing as horse meat. Nobody eats that stuff. Nobody eats horses." Remembering his four-legged companion and deceased ally, Ricardo cannot believe that heinous crimes are committed against such a fine species. Not his horse. He boots Martin in the shins to force away thoughts of his horse served up like prime ribs.

"Yeah, well I know I'm right. My mother feeds my cat horse meat and kidneys."

"Oh yeah?" Another kick for Martin's cat.

"Yeah. Stop it. You'd better cut it out. Owwww! I'm getting angry now. I'm angry now. You make me angry. Angry. Angry. Angry. We will set you on fire. We will watch you burn. Owwwww!" Martin jumps around, hopping from one foot to the other to ward off the pain.

"Okay, that's enough, Ricardo. Stop hurting Martin right NOW!"

He heaves a chair against the closet door and the mirror shatters. When he looks at the broken glass on the floor, remnants of the dissipated anger that he can't hold onto, he runs crying out of the room.

"I'll get him, Tina." Kaye goes after Ricardo who doesn't stray too far.

> *Without the weight of his anger, his body compresses. The head pushes down like a clamp into the neck. The backbone crunches into his pelvis, he shuts his ears against the cracking din of himself. If only the anger could be recalled he would wedge pieces like putty in the widening spaces to keep himself together. He is smaller and smaller as the fear rises like helium in him.*

I caution everyone away from the splintered glass on the floor, pick up the phone and call the maintenance department to assist us in glass removal—pronto.

"Don't animals eat horsemeat, Miss Tina?"

"Yes, Martin, I'm afraid they do."

"Beverly, do you know what animal this is?"

"A cow?"

"Yes, it is a cow."

"Cows have titties?"

"Yes, Beverly."

Martin laughs at the mention of unmentionables.

"Where's Ricardo?" Eva wants to know.

"He's with Kaye."

"Is he coming back?"

"Yes, he's coming back."

They return. Kaye sweeps broken glass into the dustpan held by Ricardo. Everyone watches quietly. Warren peers out from his hideaway into the silence. In the quiet, he can hear the blood throb in his temples. He remembers to breathe but won't let out the air and his stomach bloats with the impurities of living. For Warren, the purpose of life is to hide and not be seen. In light he is visible and vulnerable and that is intolerable.

April 4

Martin wants to come into the classroom with two rabbits, one under each arm but he doesn't think they'll fit through the door three abreast. So instead, Zaspirilla, with his sophisticated knowledge of biochemistry and the ephemeral, transforms three into the one. Martin then passes easily through the entranceway with two of the fluffiest, pinkest rabbit ears you've ever seen flopping on the sides of his head.

"This is the day you've all been waiting for. A chocolate marsh-mallow day. Peter Rabbit is here presenting to you—jellybeans!"

"Good morning, Martin. Thank you."

The bag of jellybeans, he drops onto my desk as his rabbit's ears flap jubilantly. Mister X is dressed in a chic double lapelled sports jacket with matching pants. He models his Easter outfit immodestly.

"I'm going to hoppity-hop in the Easter Parade. You will see me on your television."

"How ya gonna be on television?" Ricardo asks Martin.

"It's easy. I will ride up in my bunny car and into the television set." Martin shifts into fourth gear and rams into another dimension.

"Come on, Ricardo, hop into the bunny mobile and away we'll go." Ricardo sits in the jump seat.

"Rrrrrrr, look out! Look out! We're coming in for a landing. Watch out! Keep out of our way! No brakes, no brakes! The brakes are stuck. Wooooooo!" They crash onto the rug into a lettuce patch. Ricardo plays dead.

"Stand back. Let's see if he's alive. He's not moving. I think we killed him. He is killed, dead. He is gone gone gone!"

Ricardo leaps onto Martin and they tussle playfully.

"Okay, stop it. Stop now. Somebody might get hurt," Martin exclaims as the wrestling match doesn't end and Ricardo's playing is more heated.

"Chicken. Chicken. Martin's a chicken."

Breathless, Martin scurries to his feet and brushes lint from his pants.

King Zagoot's personal secretary is zagooted down. The King has decided to write his memoirs. Two versions: one for the earth people whose primitive grasp of politics and the cosmos can only be described as rudimentary if not barbaric, and one for the Zagootian market.

Within this discourse, King Zagoot is setting forth the Zagootian code of ethics and sketches of a Zagootian childhood. Of course, what would a biography be without a poetic account of his kingly life, detailed and with glossy photographs? Movie rights will be sold to Universal Pictures only.

In the second version King Zagoot will recount

his holiday in an earth prison and depict vignettes of earth life as reported to him by the prisoners. The King thanks the prison authorities, but he will not leave until the other prisoners are released to go with him.

Kaye comes in with a dozen hardboiled eggs to color. Eva and Martin sit with me for reading while Ricardo struggles with Kaye over final consonant sounds and his math paper. With her head resting sideways on the top of her paper, Beverly painstakingly traces over the letters in her name. Warren builds with the blocks. When they fall down, he pulls on his skin as if he wants to rip off chunks of human flesh to atone for his imperfections. As Kaye gets closer, Warren moves further under the desk.

Before our group story, Kaye and I find thirty uninterrupted seconds to talk.

"Tina, I just can't watch Warren hurt himself over and over. It upsets me to see a child disfigure himself like that. I don't understand how he can cause pain time after time and be okay with it. And, Tina, the scars! They'll never heal."

"I know, Kaye. It upsets me too. But I think he uses the pain as a form of stimulation. Some kids do it to primarily hurt themselves and that can also be his reason. He does it mostly, I think to feel something. Maybe that's just speculation on my part. "

"Whatever it is, you're usually right!"

"Thanks, I hope so, but it's still causing him welts and bruising."

We sit on the rug as I read the Easter story. Warren is under his desk, removed from everyone, but he seems to be listening.

After lunch, Kaye and I help everyone make Easter baskets. Eva, who has become our artist in residence, watches Kaye's demonstration and completes hers without our services. Warren cannot be coaxed out of his hideaway. Martin asks if he can make two. One he wants to send to King Zagoot for an Easter present. We layer the bottom of the basket with simulated green grass.

"Wadda we gonna put in it?"

"That's a surprise, Ricardo."

"Rotten eggs and jelly belly beans!"

"Rotten eggs?"

"Martin's kidding, Ricardo, the eggs aren't rotten. They're cooked."

"Phewy, smelly rotten eggs." Martin chants.

"Martin, if you think the eggs are rotten, you don't have to put them in your Easter basket. We'll have extra ones for someone else."

"Nope, a thousand times, nope."

We dunk the eggs in blue, green and red colored liquid.

"Look." Beverly is amazed at the wonders of science. "They colored." While the eggs are drying, Kaye fills the Easter baskets with chocolate bunnies, jellybeans and yellow marshmallow chicks. Warren gazes at the jellybeans on the table. Jellybean is a dead food. He can eat them.

Out from the safety of the desk, he heads directly to the jellybeans. Everyone cheers. Warren hears the loud noises and pauses between hiding and jellybeans. We all smile and the jellybeans urge him on.

"Here, Warren." Ricardo donates a jellybean from his own Easter basket. Warren grabs the jellybean, transfers it to his mouth, and bites down. He smiles.

"Guess what, he likes 'em." Ricardo grins at his own insight.

We pack Warren's Easter basket with jellybean on jellybean.

"Hey, is this all we get?" Ricardo whines. Somehow, he had to prick a hole in all the good that he was experiencing.

"That's all. Let's leave some room for your dinner."

"You're just cheap. You don't want us to have nothin'."

Beverly's jaw has not taken a rest from chewing. Eva picks up the blue egg in her hand and sniffs and sniffs. She's not sure what to make of it. Is it really edible? She's never seen blue food before. Her fingers remind her to shell the egg, which she does. When she peeks under the blue shell, she's relieved.

"Boiled egg," Eva announces happily.

Mister X declines. Thank you, no. He prefers poached eggs on toast.

When Warren's mom comes to take Warren home, Ricardo, by self-appointment, tells her about Warren's progress.

"He ate all 'em jellybeans."

"He did?"

"Yeah, and I gave him some, too."

"Thanks, Ricardo," says Mrs. Jackson.

Ricardo beams and I smile gratefully at Warren's mom. I'm glad that many of the parents, like Mrs. Jackson, are so attuned to these kids, not just their own, but all of them. It really helps to have their support and I know that doesn't always happen, which makes it even more special.

We clean and pack up everything while Beverly still chews and chews.

"Have a nice holiday, everybody. I'll see you soon," I call after their fleeting coats as they race out the room to catch their buses. Kaye leads the way, and Beverly, her mouth motor still chomping away at the jellybeans, holds up the rear.

> When the Easter Bunny goes to Beverly's house,
> Beverly turns all the lights on so he doesn't trip and
> so she can tell the Easter Bunny apart from any
> unwanted ghosts.
>
> Eva tells his fortune, prophesying peril, and has
> him spell his name for her a half dozen times. War-
> ren waits till the bunny leaves and gorges himself on
> jelly beans. At Ricardo's he's ambushed and robbed
> of his Easter treats.
>
> The bunny hobbles home with one enlarged
> black eye and crawls in stealthily through the bed-
> room window with Martin's assistance.

"I am so ready for this holiday!" I confide in Kaye. "I don't know why but I'm exhausted." I feign confusion.

"I know, Tina, they sure are demanding, aren't they? I feel the same way."

"And Warren—I hope he improves soon, for his own sake."

"Yeah, poor little guy! Do you mind if I leave quickly, Tina? I have to get my own kids some Easter treats or I'll hear about it forever."

"I don't mind at all. Once we're done, I'll join you."

We leave the classroom after scraping jellybeans and bits of eggshell off the carpet.

"Bye, Tina, I'll see you in a week. Have a good vacation, you hear!"

"You too, Kaye. Happy holidays!"

"Thanks," she says, unbuttoning her coat at the school entranceway.

I imagine that Kaye feels the same relief that I do as I step out of the school building and into the mild, spring afternoon, knowing that I have almost one full week to myself. Peace at last! It's some gardening time for me, if the ground isn't too hard. Nothing like a little hermetic contact with Mother Earth to sort things out. I'm also hoping to get home for Easter Sunday. Everyone's threatened to be there and I can't wait. I promised to get there early to help Mom stuff the turkey. Believe me, I'm no wonder in the kitchen, although Mom makes it seem so effortless. I live the closest to our childhood home and, truth be told, I'm probably the only one unencumbered with kids, husbands, and fiancés.

The Last Lap

April 11

"Where's Ricardo?"

"I don't know, Eva. He's probably on his way to school."

"Is Ricardo home?"

"I don't think so. He may be on the school bus."

"Is he coming to school?"

"I hope so."

"Is he sick?"

"I don't know, Eva."

"He's coming."

Ricardo is Eva's war hero. She abhors bloodshed of any sort, but she has an affinity for casualties of war. Dressed in her crisp white nurse's uniform, she will tend to Ricardo's battle wounds with courage and affection. But oh, how she wishes he would get a haircut.

Mister X holds the door open and Martin staggers in with a suitcase and a pair of bloodshot eyes. He sets the suitcase down on the floor and forlornly hangs his admiral's jacket in the closet.

"Good morning, Martin. How are you today?"

"Not good. Not good at all."

"It looks like you need some more sleep."

"You can say that again. I rocketed to Mars but the Martians were tearing each other apart and my rocket ship conked out so I had to stay there. I couldn't sleep with that racket going on. Boy, I'm never going back to Mars again."

"What's in the suitcase?"

Martin has in his suitcase: one toothbrush, one tube of toothpaste, one natural-bristle hairbrush, a fireman's outfit, an amulet, a box of crackers, one pair of handcuffs, a toy machine gun, a stick of deodorant, a fresh block of dial soap, first-aid antiseptic cream, three chocolate bars, a red-haired wig with matching beard, a stethoscope, a bathing suit, a pair of nail clippers, and one full box of Band-Aids.

"Martin, you've certainly taken a lot of things with you. Where are you going?"

"I can't tell you, Miss Tina. Sorry, but it's not allowed."

"How long do you think you'll be gone for?"

"That is hard to say. Maybe a long time, maybe not. Who knows?"

Mrs. Selby called me two days ago to inform me that Mr. Selby has temporarily moved away for a trial separation. She was distraught and very worried about Martin who's taking the separation very hard. I assured her that we'll do everything that we can to support Martin. Today, he looks exhausted but is more jumpy and animated than usual.

Mister X falls asleep at his desk before breakfast. Ricardo comes in late from a doctor's appointment, and Eva's fingers dance in excited greeting.

"Ricardo, you're back!" Martin rushes towards him with outstretched arms.

"Martin!" They embrace and fall on the floor in an arm lock.

In the afternoon, Martin shows Eva how the stethoscope works. Beverly wants to play victim, but Eva wants to listen to Ricardo's heartbeat. Instead, Beverly and Eva pull on the stethoscope until Martin halts the skirmish. Everyone is treated with Band-Aids.

"I need one for my arm." Ricardo displays an old cut. "And my finger."

"Gimme, Martin," Beverly whines.

With Eva, his head nurse by his side, Martin administers salve and bandages to all his clamoring patients. I go home with one on my left knee and one over my third eye.

April 14

"Eva, do you have something you'd like to share with us?"

"I like Ricardo."

"Aw, why did ya have to say that? Leave me alone." Ricardo wipes the hair away from his face and shifts in the chair.

"Put it on the board, Miss Tina."

"Okay, Eva."

Eva's testimony is written on the blackboard with the other news of the day.

> *The curtains she hangs in the bedroom are*
> *transparent lace. She wants the sun warm and*
> *golden on her face, as it tilts into the resplendent*
> *sparkle of morning. In the evening, she sits inside*
> *the platinum moon, strumming her mandolin and*
> *her heart.*
> *With the chords of her fingers, she sings the*
> *winking night to sleep.*

Martin's fuming! He's dismissed Zaspirilla; he doesn't trust that charlatan poking around in his business. Zaspirilla's hocus-pocus is more mumbo jumbo than Martin bargained for. Before his leave-taking, Zaspirilla gives each of us a small token of friendship. Kaye receives a pair of ear plugs, Eva finds a barrette for her hair, and Ricardo holds up his box of fish hooks. The Excedrin is mine; Beverly's is a mounted monarch butterfly. Zaspirilla bends down and gives Warren his voice box. When Martin opens his gift he brays at the disappearing figure of Zaspirilla.

April 17

"Hi, Warren."

"Hi, Warren," he repeats what I said. The words funnel coarsely through the constricted bands in his throat. Nevertheless, those are the most beautiful first words that I've ever heard.

"Hi, hi, hi, hello, hello, hello, hello, good morning, good morning."

"You seem happy this morning, Martin," I call.

"I got Nikes on my feet and shark teeth under my pillow."

"Shark's teeth?"

"Yup, see?" When Martin opens his mouth, I see a gummy space where his tooth used to be.

"Your tooth fell out! Congratulations."

"Thank you. Thank you. And the fairy canary mother is going to give me all her money."

"What will you do with all the money?"

"I will hide it in my secret cave so no one will take it."

> *Negotiations are under way in the prison strike where King Zagoot is unanimously elected to represent the prisoners. A sit-down is in effect in the northern wing and independent contractors are beginning work on the skylight. Prison fund contributions flood in from all over the universe while the interstellar forces await instructions.*
>
> *So far the demands agreed upon are prison expansion and modernization: escalators, silk sheets, Zagootian waitresses and Zagootian movies rated zg, pinball machines, and wages for time and a half. Both sides are in dispute over the retirement plan and the two-week paid vacation on Zagoot after the first year of commitment.*
>
> *Under King Zagoot's tutelage, the prisoners refuse to budge on any issues.*

Warren sits in his chair and pounds on his head while the colored chips to be sorted clink on the floor. Before anyone else has a chance to get to him, Ricardo leaves his desk and holds

Warren's hands as he has watched Kaye and me do.

"I'm not gonna let you hurt yourself, Warren. I'm stronger than ya, see, and we don't let people get hurt around here. Ya gotta stop."

Kaye and I listen to our message, now uttered by Ricardo, whose blow-ups have decreased to two times a day. No small feat. Ricardo picks up the chips for Warren and sets them on his desk.

"There ya go. Now do your work."

Beverly points to the left-over mustard packs from lunch. "Miss Tina, can I have dem?"

"What do you want them for, Beverly?"

"For hotdogs. I cook hotdogs and put on the mustard."

"You make dinner all by yourself?"

"I gotta big, big jar of mustard at home," Ricardo boasts.

"Oh yeah? I have a jar of mustard that is six feet tall and bigger than all of you."

"I got a jar of mustard home," Beverly shyly chimes in.

"If you have a jar of mustard at home, Beverly, then why do you need these?"

"I wants them."

I give Beverly the packs and she bounces back to her seat with meant-to-be-concealed crayons sticking out of her pants pocket.

"Beverly, come here to me, please."

She walks slowly back to me, her every step a tentative question.

"Where did you get the crayons from?"

"I don' oo."

"Did you take them from the crayon box?" Her eyes gaze everywhere but at me.

"I wants to play wif 'em."

"You don't have crayons to color with at home?" Beverly shakes her head and won't look at me.

"Well, you'll have to give these back and then come over to me."

Every step she turns, unbelieving. Will I change my mind? Maybe I'll relent and tell her that she doesn't have to return them. I don't and the crayons are restored to their rightful place.

"Beverly," I hold her around her shoulders. "I'm going to give you some crayons to take home with you. Crayons to play with and for you to keep. If you want something in here, you have to ask for it first. Do you understand?"

"Les."

A blue crayon, a red crayon, a yellow and a green crayon. I give them to her and she stands there just looking.

"I can have dem?"

"Uh huh."

"They mine"?

"Yes, all for Beverly."

With the blue crayon she brushes in a whorled sky over her head, and yellow spokes illuminate the shadowy edges of the earth under her feet.

The green crayon wheels tufts of grass. When she beholds the whirling crayon splendor, the red dress is on and she is dancing.

April 24

Morning work folders are completed and everyone is attentive for the morning story. Ricardo sits sprawled out on the rug with his head in Warren's small lap while Warren is placid and looks outward past all of us—somewhere.

"I like the story."

"I'll put the book in the bookshelf, Eva, and you can take a look at it when you want to. Okay, there are ten minutes of game time before we wash up for lunch."

"Ricardo, you want to play battleship with the boats?" Martin gets up, heading for the toy center in the back of the room.

"Yeah."

The plastic warships collide on the rug.

"Let 'er rip," Admiral Martin orders.

"Here she comes." The boats meet bow to bow and splash!

"Man overboard, man overboard. Hold your fire, men."

"Look out, a whale!"

"It's a shark, not a whale. Sharks kill people. This shark is gonna kill the drowning man."

"It's a whale, ya hear? This whale is gonna rip that man up. Ya see?"

"It's a shark, Ricardo. I know what it is."

"A whale, ya dumb punk."

"A shark."

"A whale."

"A shark."

"Your mother."

"Your mother."

For the retort, Ricardo knuckles Martin in the head.

"Ow! Stop it. I'll blast you." Martin raises his fists but forgets to punch. "Ow!"

"Boys!" Kaye intervenes.

"That little dummy better quit goin' around talking 'bout my mother. I'll kill 'im like nothin'."

Mister X sits next to Eva at lunch. Eva is positive that Mister X has no body odor, not even the minutest scent. When he passes her a carton of milk, she doesn't see his hands reach out and the carton drops.

"Strength in those fingers," Eva repeats the well-worn phrase and looks at me.

"Look, he ate one of 'em carrots." Ricardo supervises Warren's activities and pulls a chair up next to him for every meal.

"Warren, ya did it." Ricardo hugs him and the carrot almost plops out of the tiny mouth. Nevertheless he smiles and swallows.

"Hurray for the carrot eater. Hurray for the rabbit man. Hurray for potato chips. Here, Warren, do you want one?" Martin joins in.

"Want one?"

"Take it, my boy, take it."

Ricardo grabs the potato chip and crunches it in his mouth. Kindness goes only so far.

"It was for him!' interjects Martin, defending Warren.

"Aw, he don't want it anyway. Do ya, Warren? You don't want no dumb potato chip."

Warren is speechless.

"It's not right to take it without asking. Right, Miss Kaye?"

"That's right, Martin. You should always ask first."

"Aw, just get off my back, will ya?"

"Who wants one?" Martin offers.

Who doesn't want one? Everyone shouts at once.

"Gimme one."

"Ricardo, you had one and I want some left for me."

"Gimme one. I'm askin' ya now, see."

"And one for the Ricardo."

"Thanks, ya little squirt."

"I'm not a squirt, I'm a king."

"King? Ya just a retard."

"Oh yeah?"

"Yeah."

"Oh..." Martin surprisingly has nothing more to say.

I divert them from their endless verbal tug of war and enlist their help in clearing the table. Today is a half day for students, a conference day for teachers. I look at the slow moving clock in anticipation. Hurray for the end of the day when I can take off my shoes.

May 2

Warren's mother and I stand outside the room talking, while Warren goes inside, escorted by Ricardo.

"Have you noticed anything different in Warren in the last two weeks or so?" Mrs. Jackson asks. She's visibly distressed.

"Yes, I've noticed some improvement. Warren stays with us for a few of the group activities, he is repeating some words and now sits on a chair rather than under one," I smile.

Mrs. Jackson still looks anxious and close to tears. I guide her away from the classroom door so we're not overheard.

"He's biting himself badly at home now. He has these welts on his arm from his teeth. They're all swollen and black and blue. And the head-banging has begun again. He had stopped, but now… Our pediatrician gave him a tetanus shot in case he really hurts himself. I don't know what to do. My husband and I are both very upset. He's done this before, but now it seems that he's hurting himself worse than ever. I thought maybe something was happening in school."

"If there was, I would have notified you immediately. Warren's making progress here. The hitting, punching and other self-abusive behaviors have decreased. We've placed more demands on him and raised our expectations. He seems to be developing a positive relationship with Ricardo, which is great to see. I think the relationship is good for both of them. You saw how Warren just went with Ricardo into the classroom. This brotherliness is just what we need to bring Warren out of himself and rein Ricardo in! Also, Warren's now eating some food in school which he never did before.

"I'm sorry that you're having such a hard time with him at home though, that must be very distressing. You know, sometimes when a child makes progress in one area—such as in school, there can be backsliding in other areas. I know it can be very hard for you, but I can assure you that he's moving in the right direction at school. I think it's a good idea to speak with the school counselor, Mr. Strong. He'll be able to offer some suggestions to you and your husband to help you through this difficult stage."

"Yes, we'd like that. Thank you for telling me. Can you arrange a meeting for us?"

"Yes, of course. I'll sort that out this afternoon. I think it's time for us to meet more regularly as well. How about if I call you this evening and fill you in on the arrangements? We can plan to meet again in one week to review Warren's progress both at home and in school."

"That's great. Thank you again."

"Tina," Kaye's eyes are watery. "You won't believe what this child is doing to himself. He has these bruises all over."

"Kaye, I know. His mother just told me."

"I think it's horrible. That poor little boy is really hurting himself."

Mister X has had several replies, thanks to Aunt Flora's word-of-mouth advertising. One from an elderly gentleman, a retired Shakespearean actor, who was enthralled when Aunt Flora told him that Mister X dabbles in theatrics. He's been waiting twenty-two years to re-stage *Julius Caesar* in his Victorian living-room and to play against an actor of comparable talent. Three wholesome meals a day plus a break for tea in the afternoon and cognac after dinner was the prize offer. Rehearsals are inflexible. They will be in the evening from 7:00 PM till midnight. He's relieved to announce that he lives by himself except for a Zagootian housekeeper whom he recently hired and who is working out splendidly.

Martin marches in wearing an army helmet and four stars on his pin-striped shirt.

"Terrible news, terrible news. We are at war! But don't worry, you are in safe hands. We will fight with the enemy and will get them first."

"Who are we at war with, Martin?"

"Everybody, everybody who fights with us. We will win and then we will be happy."

The water canteen is raised to his lips and he drinks.

"Hey man, can I get some of that? Where'd'ya get that thing?"

"From my uncle. He's in the army."

"Gimme, Martin."

"Say please, Beverly."

"Puese."

"What a girl. Here."

"It good."
"That's because it's a super duper root beer special."

At the meeting, King Zagoot hands out the royal cook's rhubarb pie while Zagootian waitresses serve the assembly non-alcoholic beverages.

The prisoners' demands are all met. One hundred men have been granted permission to go with King Zagoot. The Zagootians need their King home, and he's ready to leave earth politics behind him and return.

Also, free to go is the prison warden, who has resigned his post. The royal cook has just prepared his last meal in the prison. Ninety-eight more men and then they will zagoot.

A Brother Emerges

May 5

"Ricardo, how would you like to take a good note home to your mom today?"

"Yeah."

"What do you think we should tell her?"

"Tell her I got a new reading book."

"Is there anything else?"

"That I didn't throw over no desks and didn't fight with nobody."

"I'm really pleased with everything you've done today. How about telling her about helping Warren?"

"Yeah. That I helped him with the puzzles."

"Like a big brother."

"Yeah."

> *Into the quiescent puddle, he slams down his foot. Water splashes onto his clothes. He turns the rain-soaked sod over in his fingers, pulls out the squirming worms and feeds them to a wounded starling.*

"Martin, what are you looking under my desk for?"

"Shhh, you'll scare him."

"Who?"

"Miss Tina, I can't answer now. Please, I've got to catch him."

"Your bus driver is downstairs; I don't think he'll wait forever."

"I got him. Come on, boy, let's go now."

"Martin, what's in your hand?"

"A mouse."

"What are you going to do with the mouse?"

"I'm going to let him loose in my backyard."

"Oh, that's very nice of you. Goodbye."

"Miss Tina, it ain't a real mouse. It's one o' dem rubber mouses, ya know."

"Yes, I know, Ricardo. Thanks for telling me. I appreciate it."

May 8

I can't believe the weather lately. It's been terrible: rain every day with thick grey clouds like a lid sealed shut over the sky. Where's the sun? It's not just me feeling like this; the weather is affecting the children too. We are all in need of a little dose of friendly sunshine.

"When are we gonna go outside like you promised?"

"How about on a day when it's not raining?"

"Aw, that might take forever."

"I hope not. We'd have a lot of sad people around here."

"Ricardo, do you want to play rummy?" Martin offers.

"Nah, that's a sissy game."

"Let's play with the blocks."

"Awright, but I don't want to make one of 'em dumb cabins."

"A rodeo. This will be a rodeo. Let's put the stables for the horses here." Martin's already lining up the pieces. "And now here's cowboy Ricardo riding the horse. Look at him ride, folks. He's still on the horse's back. Oh no, he's off. And the horse rides away. Whoahhh! Catch him, catch him before he escapes!"

> *'Are you ready?' he calls.*
> *'Yeah, I have to get my fish hooks.'*
> *Together they slide down the steep-sloped mountain. Martin holds the tackle box while Ricardo leads with the fishing rods.*

*As their rocks skim across the swift-weaving
water, a big silver fish bolts upward and swallows
both hooks. Together, they reel him in and watch his
glistening smooth body slap against the ground one
last time.*

*Ricardo builds a bonfire and Martin slips the
fish he's filleted onto sticks like skewers. They eat
mouthfuls of fish and burnt marshmallows till dusk.*

"Miss Tina, can I take this home?" Beverly holds up the new pencil I just gave her to practice writing the numerals with.

"Yes, Beverly. I'm glad you asked me first."

Eva hops about sniffing Ricardo everywhere he goes. Less time is devoted to expanding her vocabulary and more time is spent on Ricardo-detecting. There is something unorthodox and spicy to the scent of him, like gumdrops, which Eva finds appealing despite Ricardo's dismay.

Warren, Warren. He is the victim of his own torture. He imprints his pain on his body with his teeth and only allows Ricardo to hold his hand. No one else may touch him. When I try, his body self-destructs. With Kaye, it's the same. We may only watch the mutilation, we may not prevent it. The closer we get, wanting to ease the wounded flesh which is never given time to heal, the harder he whips himself.

When we met with Warren's parents, we suggested they get some outside help. Mr. Strong said he'll see Warren once a week if Warren will let him. Right now, Warren regards everyone outside of the classroom as a suspicious foreigner. He's just getting used to us without hiding all the time. I learned from his parents that Warren has lead-poisoning. His physician told them that it has permanently affected his growth and his brain.

Martin seems preoccupied and rather silent, which is uncharacteristic of him. Where did he go, I wonder?

All the proposals Mister X has received are considered with the care of a surgeon. Another applicant writes that he is ten years old and is running away from home. When Aunt Flora tells him that Mister X is a droll character and could make life one big guffaw, the boy composes a letter immediately. Would Mister X consider taking on one almost grown boy to live with him? He's never been outside of London and he's excited about visiting the United States. How does he go about getting a passport? If Mister X would please send him some money, he promises to repay him when he gets to America. Mister X dashes off a letter on his best stationery, thanking the child, while informing him that he is really considering a more lucrative position.

May 10

Mother's Day is around the corner. As I hand out paper, crayons, and other materials to decorate the cards, I think about the sentimental card and earrings I mailed to Mom in lieu of a visit. I just can't get there this weekend. There's so much to do to get ready for the end of the school year. Reports and scheduled IEP meetings, summary meetings with families and oh, I get dizzy just thinking about all I must do. I know she'll understand. After all, the whole clan was there for Easter and had a blast.

Warren won't make a card. However, Eva designs a card for his mom and cards for everyone else just in case they lose theirs or refuse to comply like Warren. No one else backs away from the task. Martin not only designs one for his mom but also for his aunts, grandmothers and cousins.

"She took my Bugs Bunny watch. Ow, we will get her, Beverly is gonna be sorry now. We are going to hurt her if she doesn't give it back. We are counting. One, two, three, four...," Martin singsongs.

"Here." She throws it at Martin.

"Ya betta watch out who ya throwin' things at. I'll knock your nose off," Ricardo supports Martin.

"Yes, sir, we'll knock off your nose and put it in a rocket and you'll never ever get it back."

"Shut up."

"Did you hear her? I don't believe it. That girl told me to shut up. You better shut up or I'll shut you up," Ricardo threatens.

"Okay, Ricardo, leave her alone. Martin, stop teasing Beverly and Beverly, why did you take Martin's watch?"

"She heard ya, she's just actin' like she's stupid."

"I is not."

"I thought you wanted to go outside. Let's finish the get well cards for Miss Kaye and the Mother's Day cards also. Afterwards, we can go."

I speak with Beverly again about thievery and personal belongings, developing a sense of civic responsibility, a strong character, and moral fiber, particularly during her formative years. Beverly listens with morbid interest. Will she go to jail? When she discovers that we will not send her away, she promises herself that next time she will be right in her every action and not get caught.

We finally make it through the corridors, down the stairs and out the front door. Martin holds the door open for everyone, even Beverly. The kindergartners are in the playground. Eva chats with the kindergarten teacher, asking question after question, while monster Martin roars menacingly and chases Beverly and the little children around the playground amid shrill shrieks. Hidden under the bench is Warren. Sweater over his head, hands over his ears, lying face down, he tries to burrow into the cement.

"What's your name?" Eva asks the teacher.

"Mrs. Derrick. What is your name?"

"Eva. How do you spell Mrs. Derrick?" The name is spelled both aloud and to Eva's fingers.

"Whose children are these?"

"They're my children."

"Mrs. Derrick's children."

"Yes, that's right, Eva."

When Eva smells Mrs. Derrick's purse, Mrs. Derrick's perfume and, of all things, Mrs. Derrick's feet, Mrs. Derrick frowns and quickly jumps to her feet. She and her class hurriedly abandon the playground.

"Eva, some people don't like when you sniff them. It's not polite," I advise.

"Not polite, Miss Tina? Spell polite." She doesn't wait for me but spells it aloud correctly.

"RRRRRoooaarrrrr," Martin growls after them.

"Hey, Miss Tina, did ya see me? I made a basket," Ricardo calls from the adjoining court.

"Ricardo, that's wonderful. You're a good basketball player. Keep it up."

Martin charitably pushes 'his girls' on the swings. I reach as far as my hand will stretch under the bench and Warren transfers the dead jellybean from my palm to his mouth.

May 15

"Didn't ya all hear Miss Tina callin' ya? What are ya, deaf or somethin'? Now get over here and listen." Obediently they gather around Ricardo in the circle. "You gotta all listen to me 'cause I'm older than all of yas and bigger, see. And ya gotta show some 'spect for people who's older'n you all. And ya gotta listen to Miss Tina and Miss Kaye and Miss Connie and Mr. Strong and Mr. Donahue 'cause they're older like me and ya gotta 'spect them too. Now ya see? Martin and Beverly, quit laughin', ya hear? I said cut it."

"Thank you, Ricardo!" Kaye exclaims and playfully bangs a soda can down on her desk for emphasis.

The change in Ricardo lately has been incredible. He may be a little heavy-handed in his advice and his ministrations, but his intention is good and his confidence and sense of justice are apparent. His big brother role suits him. It's amazing what a little sense of responsibility can do for a person.

More Tantrums and a Thief in Our Midst

May 20

*King Zagoot, the cook and the prison warden
parade outside the prison gates with a cheering
crowd behind them. The King is awarded a lifetime
membership to the prisoners' club, which entitles
him to all benefits.*

*It's too late when they discover that their lim-
ousine driver is a member of an anarchist group
and entirely untrustworthy. They are kidnapped and
taken to underground headquarters.*

*The King's toe is broken by the cook, who acci-
dentally drops the gold rolling pin on the royal toe.
The toe turns purple and blue and no one wants to
look at the King.*

"It's time to go back inside, everyone. The buses will be here
soon. Ricardo, you may take the bicycle back; Eva, the jump rope;
Beverly, the ball; Martin, you may bring in the wagon. Warren, you
may take this."

Warren carries the bag of jellybeans inside.

"I want to bring the bicycle. I want to do it! Not Ricardo. Me.
I hate you! I hate you!" Martin screams and throws the wagon at
Ricardo.

"Why, you little bastard. I'll…"

"Martin, it's Ricardo's turn to take in the bicycle. You had a turn
yesterday. We're taking turns so that everyone has a chance."

"I don't care. I don't care if they ever get turns. I want to take the bicycle in. It's my turn, my turn!" He sobs and runs just outside of the schoolyard. I motion to Kaye to gather everything and everyone together while I tend to Martin.

"I hate you, I hate you!" he shouts at me. "You're mean and terrible and wicked and bad. You're no good. I hate you and you'd better die. You are real bad," he sniffles as I draw closer.

"I wish I never met you. I wish I never came to this mad school. I am angry, angry, angry." Tears flow freely into the words but he doesn't move away from me.

"It's okay if you hate me, Martin. You don't have to like me. I still care about you. It's all right."

"Martin, would you like to help me take the wagon inside? Your bus is probably here by now," Kaye's offer is reconciliatory and with just the right tone; her timing is perfect.

He walks behind, and when we get inside the building, he takes in the wagon, without a word.

Martin's anger may be a result of his parents' separation which is unsettling and painful for any child to undergo. Martin is no exception. At the same time that his reality tumbles around him, his fantasies also mirror the anger and displacement that he must be experiencing. Mrs. Selby and I conferred. She's willing to be more relaxed with Martin's imaginary characters, at least for the time being, but is emphatic about Peter Rabbit's and Martin Mouse's destiny. They are not to return to the Selby home. I reassured her because those playmates haven't surfaced recently, despite the major shake-up at home.

Martin's entourage has diminished, which I attribute to his ongoing adjustment and developing inner strength. However, I'm also a realist. With what's happening at home, Martin may have a setback. If so, we'll handle that, too.

Mister X rejects all applicants. They do not fulfill his expectations, and he thinks he might fare better going into business by himself. Possibly advertising—promoting Zagootian products. For

the time being, the Selbys treat him more considerately than before, and if he avoids confrontations with Martin, life is peaceful
and predictable.

May 27

Kaye makes name tags for the children to wear around their
necks. We're going to the zoo, and it would be most unfortunate
if one of our clan were found in the monkey cage, feeding the
monkeys jellybeans, scratching the gorilla's back, or worse, trying to cram himself down the throat of a rhinoceros—without
identification.

Martin saunters in wearing his zebra costume. He wants the animals to feel right at home with him there, and what better way to
express his solidarity with the animal kingdom?

"Martin, do you think you might be too warm with that flannel
outfit on?"

"That, Miss Tina, is a very silly question. Does the lion take
off his coat? Does the polar bear take off his fur? Do the leopards
remove their spots? Do elephants willingly give away their tusks?"

I can't find anything illogical about Martin's argument from an
animal perspective.

"No, Martin, they don't. But the snake jiggles out of its skin, the
caterpillar leaves behind his cocoon, and a chicken certainly doesn't
patter around with an eggshell stuck to his neck."

I'm thankful for my fundamental knowledge of zoology and
my ability to think on my feet. Martin considers this new slice of
information.

"I think zebras are cold without their stripes."

Who knows? Martin could be right. Maybe the stripes are thermal insulators, but not in the seventy-three degree temperature and
the gorgeous summer-like weather we are now having.

"Martin, ya look goofy."

"I'm not goofy, Ricardo. I'm a wild zebra."

"Ya don't look like no wild zebra to me. Nah, ya look like ya got yer pajamas on."

"All right, everyone. We need partners before we leave."

"I want Ricardo." Eva is the first to pipe up.

"Not on your life. I don't hold no girl's hand. No way. I'm gonna take care of Warren. Right, Warren?"

"Warren."

"See, he even said so."

"Eva, I will be honored to hold your hand."

Eva giggles as she grabs hold of Martin's thick, furry-skinned paw.

"Who gonna be wit me?"

"Beverly, you can be my partner. Kaye, are we ready?"

"I hope so." She quickly stuffs the earplugs in her ears.

"Wait a minute. Does anyone have to go to the bathroom before we leave? Beverly, why don't you go? Let's everybody go," I don't want any accidents or outbursts due to full bladders.

Martin refuses; he will not slip off his skin but everyone else complies.

We all take one very noisy, bumpy bus ride to the zoo. Martin enlightens the passengers by disclosing our destination, while Warren punches himself in the seat. The riders regard us strangely enough, but when Eva sniffs the lady next to her, the woman changes her mind and stands, muttering quietly about weird uncontrollable children.

"Goodbye, goodbye," Martin calls to the people as the bus stops in front of the zoo. Some of the passengers wave, some of them sigh and some arrange to have their vision checked. Is that little boy *really* wearing a zebra costume on a school trip in this warm weather?

We couldn't have chosen a better day. The zoo is crowded with hundreds of other screeching children and befuddled adults. When Warren sees them, he runs. Warren high-tails off and away while Ricardo and I chase after him, trying to pick his blue shirt out from the mass of others. I find him on the grass by the picnic tables.

"Warren, I'm going to hold you. I'm not going to hurt you. I don't want you to get lost." He lets me pick him up and carry him in my arms back to the crew.

"Tina, we're missing Ricardo."

On the thinnest, wobbliest tree branch sits Ricardo, who refuses to come down.

"Come on, Ricardo, get down. Don't you want to see the animals?"

"I'm a monkey, a monkey, and watch me jump to that other one."

"Little boy, get down from there right now or we'll send you out of the zoo." One, he's a man; two, he wears a shiny badge; and three, he's entirely unexpected. I thank the policeman profusely as Ricardo shimmies down the tree trunk.

Kaye grabs his hand amid curses, kicks and threats. In my attempt to set Warren down on the walkway, Warren cries and belts his head. I change my mind and lift him back up to avoid any scene and internal damages. We trudge off to see the lions while the human bundle in my arms digs his nails into my back.

The lions are not outside but in the lion house. We head in, but Martin tugs on my shirt sleeve.

"Miss Tina, I don't want to go in there. Please, let's not go in there. It's dark inside and I don't want to go."

I wait in the sunshine with Warren and a relieved Martin. In the excitement, Beverly forgets that the zoo does come equipped with toilets and the seat of her pants darkens with urine. Eva is disappointed that the animals are behind bars because she can't get in for a close examination. At lunch, Martin passes around the half-peeled bananas that he claims the monkeys jocularly bequeathed him, and Kaye and I split the last two Tylenols in my bottle.

"Let's go and see the zebras," Martin announces.

"Nah, let's see the giraffes."

"We'll see both of them."

At the sea lion's pool, everyone cheers when the sea lion catches his lunch. Ricardo and Martin throw up the crackerjacks and try to catch them like caramel-coated raindrops in their open mouths. Unsuccessfully.

"Look, he got titties." Beverly points to the supine baboon idly sunning herself.

"She. She has titties." I glance to know what other ears are pointed and listening.

If there is Nirvana, Beverly has just arrived: mammary glands on exhibit—real ones. Beverly ogles without inhibition. If someone gave her permission, she'd park herself there for the rest of the day and eat her lunch in front of the cage, staring absently at the naked baboon figure.

The zebras don't pop open a bottle of champagne in greeting, but when Martin explains that we are friends, their reserve disappears and Ricardo swears that one of them winked at him. Then we all follow Ricardo so he can fulfill his curiosity about the longest and most serene of all the zoo's inhabitants. The giraffes' interest, however, is miles away; we are not tall enough to be of any consequence to them. To raise our spirits, everyone gets a balloon. Warren, afraid to hold onto his, dreads the thought of his light body lifted high in the air and his life fastened to a balloon string. His balloon floats above our heads and away.

In the children's zoo, a few lambs amble freely about until Ricardo chases after them in an attempt to grab their fleece and ride them bareback. To feed a kid goat, Beverly and Eva stick out their shaking hands with animal food, then scream and run away when the goat is close enough to get any goodies.

We have walked almost the entire length of the zoo grounds and my feet are swollen with the pressure of being trapped all this hot long day inside tight shoes. Alas, it's time to go home. Of course, Ricardo doesn't want to leave and Martin elects to remain with the zebra contingent. Beverly, our little naturalist, needs to know when she'll next be returning. She is prepared to beg, borrow, or steal a camera and take candid photographs of mammals. Everyone else volunteers to leave.

At the bus stop, Ricardo picks up pieces of a broken glass bottle and accidentally slashes his finger. Now that his finger bleeds, of course, it's our fault, we made him do it. We wished it on him because we wanted to see his blood run all over Martin's handkerchief and Kaye's blouse. On the bus, he doesn't sit near us; he pretends we're not there. Beverly is asleep, with her head on my lap and Warren squeezes my skin as though it were his own.

To illustrate to Eva how to dress cuts, Martin slides a Band-Aid on her ring finger. As we pull into the familiar parking lot, the school building looks brighter and more welcoming than it ever did, and we ascend the stairs to our 'home.'

I am relieved. Class trip relatively successful with only a few mishaps: mission accomplished. No broken bones or missing teeth, just a minor cut and overall exhaustion emanating from the whole crew. Personally, I can't wait to get home, prize off my shoes, fix myself a refreshing jug of something fruity and get out into the garden where there is just the perfect spot, under a tree in dappled sunlight, for me to settle down for an hour or so before dinner with my book!

June 3

"Can I have this?"

'This' is my one good pair of scissors.

"I'm sorry, Beverly, I can't let you take the scissors home. I'm glad you asked me. Maybe you can have something else, but the scissors we need in school. If you take them home with you, we won't have any to use here."

She stares at me. When she asks, the response is negative. It would have been easier to sneak them into her jacket pocket when no one was looking. Days may pass before anyone notices that they disappeared. By then, the scissors would be safely hidden inside her house and who would know? Or, perhaps the measly pair of scissors would be completely forgotten and we wouldn't miss them. Maybe Beverly would be so far away it wouldn't matter.

"Can I have the 'raser?"

"Yes Bev. Thanks for asking."

Martin won't take off his sunglasses all day. He insists that they help him see his work papers better than before and are invaluable tools in his cognitive thinking. The math and phonics papers are completed without a flaw so I do not dispute the obvious.

> *King Zagoot is held for ransom. The anarchists holding him want three hundred million earth dollars and the King is then free to zagoot anywhere he pleases; in fact, they wish he would.*
>
> *The King has become a royal pest, disseminating his infamous doctrines among the kidnappers. The loose organization is splitting into factions, and all because of his 'more heaven than hell' speech.*
>
> *Everyone wants a slice of the pie, particularly if the royal cook is baking it.*

During playtime, Beverly chooses the viewfinder.

"Let's share," Eva suggests when she discovers what Beverly has. Beverly hands over the viewfinder to Eva. Sharing appeals to Beverly's vision of communal property and is rooted in the friendship which escaped her for so long. Eva firmly believes that sharing means I get to look at it as long as I want and you get to look at it as long as I want, too—without exception.

"Give it back. I wants to see."

"No, wait. We are sharing."

"You is looking. I wants it now."

"No, no, wait a minute. Then you can share." Eva and Beverly disagree on temporal issues. Eva's minute lasts one lifetime while Beverly's is the time it takes to count to one.

"I wants it now!" Beverly screams close to Eva's face, raising her hands to grab it away.

"I don't like you, Beverly. I don't like you anymore."

"What's this, what's this all about, girls? Say you're sorry and take it back. We are one big happy family, and families are not supposed to fight. They are supposed to like each other and never leave each other. Come on now. Everybody be friends and make up. Kiss and make up and everything will be great!" Martin unclasps the viewfinder from Eva's bewildered fingers and saunters away from the warring parties. The girls stare silently after him.

"Thank you very much, Martin. I'm assuming you've taken the viewfinder so you can put it on my desk. Isn't that right?"

"Sure thing, Miss Tina." Martin puts down the viewfinder, looking at it the entire time. I know he had something different in mind, but I also know that he likes to please and practice upstanding behavior.

June 7

"Beverly, finish your work, please."

Now Beverly's staring at me belligerently. This is a first. I've had vacant expressions and confused looks from Bev, but never a challenging one like this. Is this the same little girl, who once upon a time doubted her own shadow, now glaring back at me with her arms folded tightly across her chest?

"Finish your work first and then you may have play time."

"No. I is not."

"You're not going to finish your work or you're not going to have play time?" I ask.

"No, I is not doin' it. I is not."

Beverly sits straighter in her chair. She stares right at me. Her arms are stretched tightly across her body in refusal. Sometimes, I'm amazed at how these children progress and how that progress shows up in their lives and in our classroom. For Bev, her sense of self is stronger now and the boundaries between her and her mother are more defined. Some of the guilt and fear are lifted, guilt and fear of unspeakable demons that terrorize. She believed or was told, that something she did, fired-up their fury. That's why they come after her, but not as often as they used to. Now, Bev doesn't believe she's bad and at least she has the courage and enough ego strength to defy me. This is progress.

I'm not angry, just amused and pleased with the way she's grown here and in such a short time. Beverly must feel secure and trusting enough to challenge me. In the past, she tiptoed around me and everything, as though punishment and reproach lurked in every corner.

"Is there any reason why you don't want to do it?"

"No. I is not." Proudly she puffs out her chest and wonders what I'll do next. I wonder the same thing and do nothing. She releases refusals on the world in fearless protest. Let her savor the moment.

Eva's writing paper is covered in stars—one I put on and the others Eva penciled in.

"Eva, would you like to hang your paper up on the bulletin board?"

"Hang Eva's paper up, Miss Tina."

"It's such a neat paper. I'm very proud of you."

Eva's sentences usually slope off the paper onto the desk. Not this time. Eva walks up to my desk, holding her writing paper against her chest. "Here Miss Tina," she extends her hand with the paper out to me and I take it.

"Thank you, Eva. Let's hang it together, shall we?"

"I love you." Eva looks at me and then quickly turns away, averting her eyes.

She did look at me; I smile inside. Moments like these are priceless, flushed with pride and caring for her and her accomplishments.

"And ya gotta hang up mine 'cause I did it all and I got it all right this time." Ricardo's voice startles me and I return from my reverie.

"Ricardo, your paper's got a hole in it. Miss Tina is hanging up good papers. Not holey moley ones."

Leave it to Martin to know just how to jab Ricardo with just the right blows to rile him up. If I ever thought this day would be peaceful and that I would bear witness only to wondrous child achievements and outstanding demonstrations of progress, I was monstrously mistaken.

"There ain't nothin' wrong with this paper. So it's got a hole in it? So what? I did it, didn't I? Yer dumb head's gonna have a bigger hole in it if ya don't shut up."

"Shut up. Don't say shut up, Ricardo." Eva's fingers flutter unhappily.

"Oh no, I've really had it with this bunch of loony tunes. Now a girl thinks she can tell me what to do. I heard everything. Everybody here better shut their mouths 'cause nobody tells me what to do. Ya all hear? None of you is my mother. So shut your big fat ugly mouths or I'll shut 'em for yas. I'm warning ya. Don't make me shut 'em. I will."

Does he protest too much? Ricardo looks at the hole his eraser chewed and tries to patch it up by wetting his fingers and pushing the curling paper out to lengthen it. It doesn't work. His mouth secretes saliva, not paper glue.

"Ricardo, let's see if we can fix up the hole," I offer.

He brings the scotch tape and on the underside of the paper we flatten down a strip of tape and patch up the paper.

"See, ya dummies, there ain't no hole now. Yer lucky, I woulda pulled all ya pants down and whipped your butts."

The description of Ricardo's aborted retribution magnifies across Martin's movie screen speeded up and in reverse. Martin giggles.

"Is you gonna hang up my paper?" Beverly questions.

"How can I, Beverly? It's not finished yet. I'm only hanging up papers that are done. Finish yours and I'll put it up with the others."

Beverly looks down at the blank paper, up at the bulletin board, and hatefully at me. She rubs her dry lips, chews tirelessly on the pencil eraser but works.

"I don't like you, Miss Tina," Beverly whispers.

Now, where have I heard those words before?

"What a thing to say to Miss Tina," Kaye interjects. "You'll hurt Miss Tina's feelings if you say things like that."

"It's really okay, Kaye, Beverly doesn't have to like me. I still like you, Beverly."

"I like you, Miss Kaye. But I don't like Miss Tina."

The paper is finally finished and Beverly hands it to me without a word.

"Thank you, Beverly. Your work looks very nice."

I think about the effort these kids have endured every day just to complete their papers or tasks. So many small activities that once turned into major catastrophes remain just tasks to complete now. They're still challenging to my children, but less so and somehow we get through them quicker. The outrages have lessened, most of the time, since the start of school. Yes, the effort, often accompanied by complaints or dissent continues. These days, more likely, I'm presented with veritable finished products. And oh, the effort a teacher endures to receive these scholarly gifts is nothing to scoff at. Sometimes, the mental and physical exhaustion I feel at the end of the day is off the charts. Sometimes—now that's an understatement.

Countdown to Summer Vacation

June 12

Martin jingles two piggy banks in the air.

"I'm rich. I'm rich. I'm going to take all the money out of my banks and give it away to the people who want it. Then everyone will clap for me."

Martin bows, but his Robin Hood outfit is too tight and it splits.

"Oh no, this is terrible. I need magic fingers, I need super glue, I need ..."

"You need to quit eating so much devil's food cake, fatso."

Ricardo circles Martin and points at the hole in Martin's pants. "Martin's got a big fat hole in his pants. Dumbo, Martin!"

Ricardo believes his friend's misfortune is the most hilarious event he's ever witnessed; he laughs raucously.

"You," our philanthropist shouts, "need to keep your monkey out of my business or I will crush him."

"Who ya gonna crush, wise guy? Huh, huh, ya little baby, who?" Ricardo leans in menacingly and Martin hurls one of the piggy banks at Ricardo's feet.

"Now look what you made me do, Ricardo. Now look at what you've done."

"Me? Ya threw the dumb bank down yourself. I didn't put a finger on that bank. Ya broke it yourself. So don't go blaming me, 'cause I didn't touch your stupid bank. And who cares that ya saved up your money, anyway? I don't, for sure."

Eva, Beverly and Ricardo scramble on the floor to pick up the coins.

"Give them back. You better not steal any 'cause we will send you far away and you'll be lost in space forever. Miss Kaye, Miss Tina, they're taking my money. Give it to me, now."

Kaye hands Martin an envelope for the spilled coins. As everyone gathers them up, Beverly observes me watching her and changes her mind. Kaye reprimands Martin for throwing school materials carelessly aside as he searches for the missing coins. Together, they clean up the broken clay remains of the piggy bank scattered all over the floor.

"But Miss Kaye, I had to do it. I just had to. That money is the answer to everything. And besides, Ricardo's in real trouble now. He's going to get it."

> *King Zagoot sends a taped message to planet Zagoot and the interstellar forces, telling his people not to worry; the King is well and his toe is healing. The swelling is down and he can easily exercise it.*
>
> *If they can't raise the money to send to these despots, he will understand and hold no grudge against anyone, anywhere. He sends his love to the Zagootian children and the cook sends regards to his wife.*
>
> *King Zagoot urges them all to be brave in such a difficult time and space as now.*

"Martin, would you like me to lock the money, bank, and the envelope up in my closet for safekeeping? That way we will be sure it doesn't get lost."

"I don't know, Miss Tina. If anything should happen to this we will all be dead."

"Martin, I assure you, nothing will happen to it if it's in the closet. At the end of the day, you may take it home again."

After consulting with Mister X, Martin and I lock up our fate in the closet. Warren finds a penny under his desk and licks it. Coins

are dead, but they don't crunch easily. Kaye rescues the penny just
in time.

June 14

Now is the time to prepare the children for the changes to follow.
"There are only eight more days of school left and then we'll
have summer vacation."

"What's gonna happen to us?" Ricardo demands.

"You'll be home from school, riding your bicycle, going to the
beach and swimming."

"Aw, I don't go nowhere. I just hang around the house and do
nothin'. We might as well go to school 'cause I can't go nowhere
anyway."

"I can go wherever I like and no one will know where I am,"
Martin exclaims.

"How ya gonna do that?"

"I will do it!" Martin is wary to disclose any more details than
are necessary.

"September, we come back?" Eva looks at me for reassurance.
Her hands flap excitedly.

"Yes, in September everyone will come back to school."

"Are we gonna be in this class?"

"Yes, Ricardo. You and Eva and Martin, Warren and Beverly
will come back to the same classroom."

"I'm gonna stay in this class till I'm twelve years old," Ricardo
boasts.

Three more years of Ricardo is not exactly what I had in mind,
but I acknowledge his enthusiasm.

Mister X shuffles through his work papers nostalgically and
stuffs the ones he wants to take with him into the attaché case. His
actions incite the jitters in everyone. Martin paces up and down the
aisles. Eva spins in the middle of the room, while Ricardo curses the
day he ever set eyes on the place.

"First ya tell us we can't leave and now yer tellin' us to get lost."

"Ricardo, I'm sad about leaving all of you too, but we're going to see each other again. We still have eight days before school closes and we have all next year. I'll miss all of you, and then we will be together again."

"Nah, ya don't mean it. Ya won't miss nobody. I ain't gonna feel bad, that's for sure. I'll be glad when school's over, then I won't have to look in all your dumb stupid faces no more. Yeah, I'll really be happy then. You can bet on it." Ricardo kicks his workbook around the room and turns over chairs for emphasis.

"Is you gonna be back here, Miss Tina?"

"Yes, Beverly, I'll be right back here in room 207 next year."

"I likes you, Miss Tina."

"I know you do, Beverly, even when you don't tell me."

Beverly hugs me. I try to explain to them that we have eight full days left to the school year, but they turn down their hearing aids, adjust the dials in their facial apparatus to 'gloom' and set their energy gauges to off.

June 20

Martin's beach ball bounces into the room first. It is followed by a snorkel, and Martin emerges dressed in his scuba diving outfit. Eva sniffs to her heart's content. The water on our rubberized Martin smells like the Gulf Stream and Martin is the essence of a freshwater fish.

"Are you going diving after school, Martin?"

"I have returned from an underwater adventure you wouldn't believe."

Probably I wouldn't. "What adventure is that?"

"I have been diving for lost treasure, and I have found something to make your ears burn."

I can hardly wait.

"Last night when all of you were asleep, I was on board a big ship. It was hard to see, it was nighttime, and I dove down, down, down into the freezing cold water and found it."

"Martin, what did you find in the water?" Suspense is prolonged as Martin demonstrates his diving skills from an imaginary deck. He swishes around in the water with his flippers flouncing about on the floor.

"A treasure chest. I jammed it open with my knife, and inside I found gold, gold! And this."

Martin hands the papers to me. One yellowing treasure map copied in a child's hand, and one homework paper.

"Thank you, Martin. Your homework is very well done."

"Where's all the gold ya found? If ya found gold how come ya didn't bring it in to school? 'Cause ya lyin'. Stories, that's all ya ever tell is make believe stories. Nothin' ya say is true. You just act crazy like some nut. Why should I be friends witcha? Ya losin' all yer marbles."

"I don't have marbles in my head I have brains. Here."

Martin flips a gold piece to Ricardo, who respectfully shuts up. Kaye touches her forehead to determine if she has a fever, and I blink my eyes, hoping the gold nugget isn't really there at all. Mister X comforts each of us with a glass of Perrier from his thermos.

June 22

"It's time to take some of your belongings home with you. Martin, you have many things in the closet—your suitcase, your umbrella, your flippers, your jogging suit, your asbestos blanket and more."

"Miss Tina, if you don't mind, I think I'll leave those things here for next year when I come back."

"If you're sure you want to do that, Martin, it's all right with me."

The ransom is paid by a universe representative,

who prefers to remain anonymous. King Zagoot and
the royal cook are released to the interstellar forces.
  In their glee, the anarchists sit on their wealth
and celebrate with the royal cook's anniversary
cake. Their eyes are so taken with dollar bills that
they are blinded to the phosphorous color of the
icing and keel over into the lucre, dead with food
poison.
  The ransom money is swiftly returned to the
monarchy. King Zagoot and the royal cook zagoot
to planet Zagoot, amid farewells and photographs.
  After his rest, King Zagoot promises the weep-
ing crowd he will return on an earth visit but first he
must put his planet in order.

"Martin, don't ya want to take home your sunglasses?"

"Nah, if you want them, Ricardo, you can keep them."

"Hey, thanks, man." With the sunglasses on, Ricardo stumbles into desks and chairs. Mister X lends Ricardo his walking stick and Eva gives him a tin cup. A gold coin clinks into the cup from nowhere.

  He rubs his eyes and crystalline yellow stars
rise to greet him. The moon unwinds her silver
tresses and Ricardo climbs the silky lattice to sleep
inside her softly lit arms.

June 24

"Come on, Warren, Miss Tina wants everyone to sit at the table." Ricardo helps Warren put the pegs back in the box.

"Ladies and gentlemen, we are proud to say today is a mother-father-sister-brother-grandmother day."

"We only have a few hours before your parents arrive. We have to hurry." The tablecloth is spread by Eva and Kaye. Ricardo and Martin, our local heroes, carry in all the chairs.

"What we gonna make?"

"We're going to make tuna fish sandwiches and a salad. Kaye, did you remember the bowl?"

"Yes, Tina."

"Ricardo, you may open all the cans. Where's the bread?"

"He's got it."

"Warren, give me the loaf of bread. Here, you may have a piece."

"Eva, would you like to put the tuna fish in the bowl?" Eva sticks her nose into the tuna flakes.

"Oh, no, she's gonna mess it up. Now look what she's doin'."

"Eva Kineva, get your rosy nosy out of the tuna fish. I command you!" orders Martin.

"All right, who wants to put the lemon in? Beverly?"

"I want to, Miss Tina. I want to put the lemon in. It's my turn to put the lemon in. I can't wait forever. I want to do it now-ow-ow!" Martin's tears leak onto his plum-colored shirt.

"Aw, let him do it, Miss Tina," Ricardo, his friend and ally, gestures in support at Martin and his copious tears.

"Martin, you may have a turn after Beverly." At this rate we're going to have a very lemony salad with only a hint of tuna fish. "Ricardo, would you put the mayonnaise in for us?"

"Yeah!"

The sandwiches are made and Beverly and Eva take turns to wash out the bowl.

"Martin, do you remember your speech?"

"I will never forget it!" He's right about that. It's recorded on his automatic reel-to-reel—permanently.

> *King Zagoot dispatches a letter to Mister X. Planet Zagoot is more beautiful than ever, the flora and sunsets are a sight for Zagootian eyes. The Zagootian children are well and send their love to the earth people.*

King Zagoot is tickled to report the children are learning Earthlingese as though it were their own language.

A shipment of Zagootian folklore and his completed memoirs will zagoot down for Mister X to market. All proceeds are to be zagooted up immediately.

"We have time to put the refreshments on the table. I need helpers." Four volunteers. Warren sits alternately punching himself and sucking on bread crust.

"Ricardo, don't you think it would be nice if you combed your hair?"

"I ain't got no comb."

"Here, I'll lend you mine."

In the bathroom he slicks down his hair and scrubs his hands and his face.

"How do I look now?"

"Ricardo, you are one of the cleanest, handsomest boys I've ever seen."

"You outdid yourself this time, Ricardo. I didn't recognize you." Kaye smiles and he glows.

The parents arrive. Eva ushers her mother in, waving her arms and fingers excitedly. Through the doorway walk Mrs. Selby, Aunt Harriet and Uncle Otis. Thankfully, Mr. Selby is with them, just lagging a little behind. Today of all days is important to show a united front. All the parents are friendly and polite with each other, shaking hands, nodding and smiling. Martin directs them to the arranged seats and they willingly follow his instruction. The fact that they're here, and their children have made it through the year, with everyone intact and no threats of expulsion and some academic achievement, are the miracles they're here to celebrate. They come together and break bread to commemorate this moment and to honor their children. Martin does us proud as he demonstrates just the right amount of authority and friendliness to the parents, while he guides them inside. Of course, we rehearsed many times and he learned his part splendidly.

"Ladies and gentlemen..." Martin looks over at me and I nod with encouragement for him to continue.

Beverly giggles and Kaye gently touches Bev's shoulder to silence her.

"SShh! We welcome you to room 207 and thank you for coming." Martin bows and his valedictorian hat slips over his eyes. "Hanging all over the room, are some of our best work. Please take time to look at the papers. We worked hard this year. We hope you are proud of us, because we are proud of us and proud of you, too. And, we even made snacks, but Miss Tina said we can't have them 'til the end, so you'll have to wait. Sorry, sorry." Martin bows again, stirred on by the applause and laughter. What's a little ad-libbing anyway? It certainly hasn't diminished the mood; on the contrary, everyone is eager.

Applause, applause. Warren holds his mother's jacket over his ears.

"It is time for the awards. Everyone take your seats." Martin steps aside to give Kaye room in the center to announce the awards.

"The first award goes to Eva for reading." Kaye looks at Eva who rushes up from her seat. Eva sniffs the parchment.

"Our next award is for Ricardo, a 'big brother' award for all his help. Come on, Ricardo," Kaye calls softly when he doesn't budge.

"Me?" He looks utterly flabbergasted.

"Yes, you, Ricardo. Come up to the front of the room and get it." Ricardo trips over Mrs. Crimp's purse as he comes to the front of the class, still looking shocked, although his eyes beam with pride.

"And for Beverly we have an award for sharing." Beverly jumps up. She smiles and grabs her certificate, clutching it closely to her chest with an urgency that says 'mine!'

The next award is for showmanship and it goes to Martin." The clapping is thunderous. "For Warren we have an award for bravery."

Mister X receives a prize for his dapper appearance. He straightens his carnation to accept the medal. Everyone claps. Everyone, that is, but Martin who whistles heavenly.

"Ladies and gentlemen, lunch is now served. Keep your seats on, and we will fill up your plates with hasty tasty tuna fish." Martin once again faces the small group of parents and bows.

"What's your name?" Eva asks Beverly's mom at the makeshift buffet table we created in the back of the classroom.

"Mrs. Crimp." She helps Eva put a tuna fish sandwich on her plate.

Do you want another plate and sandwich for your mom, Eva?" Mrs. Crimp asks.

"Yes, Mom sandwich. How do you spell Mrs. Crimp?" Eva's fingers trace the letters in the air as Mrs. Crimp spells them aloud for her. Eva takes the plates that Mrs. Crimp extends to her and bounces back to her mother who is busily talking with Miss Kaye.

Warren sits in his mother's lap with two slices of bread, one for each hand, while Martin gazes dreamily into his salad bowl. When it's time for the parents to leave, Martin and Ricardo accompany them to the door. The party must have been a great success because every tuna fish sandwich is eaten up, discounting the soggy one in Beverly Crimp's pocket.

"I want to go, too. I want to go!" Eva screams as she watches all the parents, her mom included, leave the class.

"Now, Eva, we must wait for the bus. Your bus is coming."

"No bus, no bus, Martin. I want to go hommmmmme."

"Home? Did you say home? Well, step right into my home machine, and we will flip you home in a jiffy. Come on!" Eva has heard that story before, and she is not about to be taken in again.

"Take me home, Martin."

"All right, Beverly, get in but don't sit on my hat. Away, away, away we zip into the wild blue."

June 28

"What's wrong, Ricardo?"

"Nothin'."

"I thought you wanted to go to the playground with us. You've been talking about going outside all year. Here's your chance."

"Yeah."

"I really need your help with the bicycle. Do you think you can take it out for me?"

"Uh huh."

"Good. Martin, hold onto your wagon. Let's go." They look at me as though I speak a foreign language. No one moves.

"What's going on around here?"

"Is we gonna have school 'morrow?"

"No, Beverly, today is the last day of school."

> *Since it's their last day they agree to do nothing. Ricardo ties up the teachers with the jump rope. Beverly and Eva struggle with their cargo of two teachers while Martin points the gun.*
>
> *Warren stones us with jellybeans. They wheel us to the monkey bars and leave us there.*
>
> *From the sandbox they heap buckets of sand into Ricardo's Cadillac and ride off to the beach.*

From our outpost, Kaye and I marvel at the children's world. It's amazing, watching this group interact together and bearing witness to the relationships that have formed in our midst—the roles and the status that each child holds. Their emotions are running high today; they're leaving school for a while and the safe routine of loathing, fighting, loving and sharing highs, lows, successes, pain, and joy is coming to a close, for now. I don't see the glee of the last day of school in the eyes of these children, just uncertainty of the unscheduled days that lie ahead.

Unlike the other children in the school who are flying high with the imminent summer vacation, my kids are having trouble adjusting to this change and to saying goodbye, even if it's only for a short time. The end of the school year is another disappointment to them and is registered in their voices, expressions, attitudes and farewells. My observations reflect back to me in Ricardo's words and the conversation that follows them.

"Ya just want to get rid of us. I told ya so. They don't like us. They don't care 'nothin' about us. They wouldn't care if we was dead."

"Is we dead?"

You can always rely on Bev as the voice of the existential.

"Nah, but a lot they care. All they care about is gettin' their money and goin' on vacations. I hate this joint and I'm never comin' back. You'll see."

"Me neither. They can miss us all day long and all night too. I'm never ever stepping inside this rabbit hole again," Martin agrees.

"I'm sorry you boys feel that way about our classroom. I'm going to miss every one of you very, very much. I'm looking forward to seeing all of you next year and having you all in my class again."

"Yeah, well ya can forget it." Ricardo is adamant, turns his back to me, and presses his hands over his ears to silence me.

"That's right. Just forget it. Forget about everything."

"I know I won't forget anyone here and I'll miss you," I reassure them.

"What a liar she turned out to be. Didn't she, Martin? What a liar. Ya can't trust nobody. Come on, let's blow up the cars."

I know they don't really mean the hateful words that discount all the good that we've accomplished here and all they've learned to feel, such as trust, friendship and yes, even pride. It's just their way to release steam and express disfavor with having to leave and face the long days of summer separation and maybe even isolation. Goodbyes are never easy, even when they're temporary. What I find wonderful is that they are sharing their dislikes and over-the-top sentiments with each other, just like friends do. They band together to complain and rail against the perceived injustice of school's end like all children and it seems the most natural thing in the world.

"Watch out for the fire! Stand back, everyone. The cars are exploding into a million zillion bumper sticker pieces. Here we go!" Kaye puts the imaginary flames out with the play fire extinguisher and I sweep up the hot scraps of metal off the rug.

"Eva, your bus is here."

"Noooooooooo! Noooooooooo!" Eva throws her notebooks on the floor.

The phone rings again. "And Ricardo, your bus driver is in the office. Come on." I hug a tearful Eva. Beverly cries when she sees Eva weeping.

"Goodbye, Ricardo, have a good summer." Ricardo slams the door. Poor Warren hasn't removed his hands from his ears all day.

"Bye Miss Tina, Miss Kaye. Thanks for everything." Martin shakes our hands. "I'm going on vacation."

"Come on, Beverly, let's wipe your tears. Here, "Goodbye. Goodbye."

With all the children gone, Kaye and I finish taking down the decorations. A knock on the door reveals Mister X returning for his forgotten derby. He blots his eyes with his handkerchief and leaves a book on my desk. Curiously, I sit down and leaf through his first major work: *A Zagootian Fairytale*.

And they are gone. The children who have been the cornerstone of my world for the past nine months have left. I am pleased with all we've achieved. I can see the changes and the growth that's taken place in each child. Even Warren has made a little progress. Some semblance of a cohesive class has emerged and I wonder what will happen when they return. Will we be able to begin where we left off or will it feel like starting all over again? I hope not, we've come too far. There'll be more new children entering our classroom, which, of course, will make a difference. A new pecking order will emerge, new roles, new personalities, quirks and behavior for everyone to adjust to. I only hope that the foundation that we've built is strong enough, and will hold up under the strain of new admittances, unexpected surprises and summer partings. Tina, stop ruminating about next September. I have time before I have to think about all that, all summer in fact, just not today!

The place is still, the air in the classroom is taking its first vacation breath. The dust is hovering, about to settle anew, like the dust that dances momentarily in the air in the wake of a passing truck on a dry dirt road. Kaye and I too, are just exhaling. Has it been ten months since I last did that, exhale fully, emptying my lungs, letting it all out? I can't remember. These children and this space have been my breath. They have sustained me and I have literally breathed with them, of them, from them, and for them since my very first meeting with twirling Eva back in March of last year.

"Tina, I think that about does it," Kaye stretches upward, crepe paper and streamers, pulled down from the walls and bulletin boards, lie in her hands. "I don't know about you, but I'm going home, get in my jeans, mix-up a cocktail and grin. Alan and I've arranged for the kids to sleep over at their cousin's and we're going to have an entire evening, just the two of us." She beams at me and we hug, laughing and almost giddy at the idea of being so fancy-free.

"Kaye, I know you don't take compliments easily, or at least not a lot of them all at once, so I'll be brief. I truly want you to know that I don't think I could've done all this without you and I'm very grateful." I give her a bouquet of lilacs straight from my garden, kept cold all day in the staff lounge refrigerator.

"Tina, thanks, they're lovely." Kaye leaves first. I linger; I want the few remaining minutes in the room all to myself just to savor what took place here and breathe in the memories.

As for the summer, well, I have to see what the next days of breathing in and out will bring. I already have some plans, family to see, friends to visit, places to go, and my art. How long has it been since I sketched anything or even thought about painting? Probably close to a year. Unbelievable! The last masterpieces I worked on were completed last summer and they were of my lovely garden. I vow to make time during the next school year for my art. It's not that my creativity isn't actively working with these kids, just the opposite. I've had to stay on my toes and be able to conjure up anything at a moment's notice while remaining calm and levelheaded. Of course, we've had make-believe and the unusual for counterbalance.

My mind wanders back again to summertime as I close the door of room 207 and lock it behind me. Once in the office, I turn in my keys and final papers; the school ending is now official. I hug Rita, the secretary, who always helps me out. In the warm outdoor sunlight, I breathe in my new freedom and the lazy days ahead of me. Knowing me, they won't be so lazy, but certainly a well-earned break from the former hectic routine.

There'll be overdue massages to indulge in, and my garden to tend and nurture once again. Perennials are wonderful; they spring up like magic, year after year to delight and mesmerize. I love a garden of my very own. A garden where the flowers grow with and through the weeds and where there is nothing, nothing that is untouched by the light of the sun. Here in my garden is a special sacred place, a veritable kingdom that is more heaven than hell.

Epilogue

The Philadelphia Experiment

This fictional work is based on a real experiment in the Philadelphia school system. Mandated to respond to the Education for the Handicapped Act (EHA) of 1975), now called the Individuals with Disabilities Education Act (IDEA), schools had to develop programs and classes for children who were once deprived public education. Because of my assigned job to pioneer the special program and my close contact with these kids, I was initially given a cool welcome by the faculty. They needed time to understand how the school and everyone would be affected. It was an additional educational headache for which many were ill-prepared and wanted no part of. Few believed the program would work, and if votes were taken at that time, many people didn't want it to be successful. Parents of children that already attended the school were also wary of the impact that this program would have on their own children's education. Doubts and fears ran high.

Although many of the educational practices current today include other methods for teaching children with special needs and children on the autism spectrum, the successes of the pioneer program cannot be underestimated. These children grew, learned, and gained confidence and self-acceptance to move forward in their lives and embrace their ability to learn and be loved.

Before the mandate, many children were kept at home and home schooled, if they were lucky. More often, their fate was one of isolation. Their parents had to find their own way without support from the educational system. Many medical professionals were discouraging and non-supportive and recommended institutional-ization to the families. Parents who dissented to send their children away weren't adequately equipped to teach their children at home. Often, they had no other choice. They were forced to make do while public education was free and open to all the other children in their community, their state and their country.

School administrators only had to say that a child was too 'handi-capped' to be educated and the schools were let off the hook without much accountability. Public sentiment mirrored the views of the edu-cational system. Keep these children hidden and apart from the rest of us because it was less uncomfortable than if they had to be seen and interact with other people. It was easier to pretend that these kids didn't exist. If they weren't seen or heard, that pretense could be upheld.

Sentiment slowly changed as parents fought timeless battles to force a change in outdated laws to allow their children to be ed-ucated and to participate in the mainstream. Children who hadn't been seen because of their parents' own embarrassment, public fear, ridicule, or lack of acceptance were becoming visible and we had to get used to it. Now the onus was on schools to accommodate the new law and the children waiting on the sidelines to be served. An educational system had to be functionally designed that was fair and ultimately successful for the children.

Many states had laws that explicitly excluded children with certain types of disabilities from attending public school, including children who were blind, deaf, and children labeled "emotionally disturbed" or "mentally retarded." At the time the EHA was enacted, more than 1 million children in the U.S. had no access to the public school system. Many of these children that were living in state institutions received limited or no educational or rehabilitation services. Another 3.5 mil-lion children attended school, but were "warehoused" in segregated facilities and received little or no effective instruction. [1]

Schools took time to respond with concrete programs. Administrators were understandably nervous and unsure how to

[1]   https://en.wikipedia.org/wiki/Individuals_with_Disabilities_Education_Act

proceed. There was no precedent for what was happening—this was it. How to educate these children in public education was the new challenge. The how would hopefully and painstakingly be forthcoming. The now for school districts was compliance with the federal law.

Special Education Is Here to Stay

The country's late 70s pioneering efforts have succeeded in establishing Special Education as a standard part of public education. About 95 percent of school-age children and youth ages 6–21 who were served under IDEA in 2012–13 were enrolled in regular schools. The percentage of children served under IDEA who spent most of the school day (i.e., 80 percent or more) in general classes in regular schools increased from 33 percent in 1990–91 to 61 percent in 2012–13.[2] Children who had been rejected previously from K-12 public schools are now an integral part of this country's educational system. Upon certification from public school many of these children attend college or become trained vocationally so they can enter the job market later on.

June 24, 2014 marked another landmark initiative for students with disabilities – Results Driven Accountability from the U.S. Department of Education. For the first time in IDEA's history, states were rated on how well they implement IDEA by combining compliance with student outcomes.[3]

One of our greatest fears is fear of the unknown. Children who had been isolated and rejected have demonstrated remarkable courage. They are to be commended for giving themselves permission to risk potential ridicule and bullying from their peers, and misunderstanding from well-meaning adults. I also applaud their parents whose tireless efforts were and still are instrumental in creating educational and legislative changes for their children.

---

[2] http://nces.ed.gov/programs/coe/indicator_cgg.asp
[3] http://www.cec.sped.org/News/Special-Education-Today/Need-to-Know/
Need-to-Know-IDEA-RDA

Although progress has been made, much more needs to be done to truly integrate these children and young adults into the mainstream of education, work and life.

The Celebration of Uniqueness

Could it be possible that children who are different are endowed with extraordinary talents? We have many examples of artists, scientists, writers and other innovative individuals who were considered misfits. If we give every child an opportunity to develop their gifts and if we include these children in our public education model, are we not delivering a greater service to society and humankind than if we continue to isolate them?

Over the years, as our society developed greater acceptance of and respect for diversity, many educators have come to celebrate 'differences' as special gifts. They started to ask why every child should be forced to adapt to one standard or method of learning. The term 'different' could be perceived as an asset instead of a liability.

Rudolf Steiner,[4] Maria Montessori,[5] and many other pioneers of education have addressed the issue of difference from fresh perspectives. They applauded the unique differences of each child as vital to individual development. Their educational slant included experiential learning, the arts and social skills as well as academics as an integral or organic part of a child's whole being or 'total person' experience.

When I first decided to write this book, I approached many mainstream publishers. They told me outright that they wouldn't consider the possibility of publishing a book whose main characters were children with disabilities. The hidden message was: "If we pretend these aberrations don't exist, they will go away." Or: "What people don't know won't hurt them. At least we can pretend we are all alike so there's some kind of norm."

[4]   http://en.wikipedia.org/wiki/Waldorf_education
[5]   http://en.wikipedia.org/wiki/Maria_Montessori

Fortunately both denial and deception had an expiration date. Along came the film *Rain Man* in 1988 that paved the way for the media and the community to open up and include the invisibles into life and art.

My Personal Rewards as a Special Education Pioneer

From a personal standpoint, perhaps the most valuable reward for participating in the Philadelphia Special Education pioneering program was the discovery of my ability to enter these children's worlds and successfully interact with them at their level. Play, imagination, and acceptance were the gateways to reaching them. I also imagined crawling inside their minds to listen and understand their feelings and experiences. At one time or another, we've all experienced fear, anger, self-doubt, pain, and maybe even rejection, as well as joy, love, and accomplishment. I relied on my memory and the memories of people I coached and counseled to describe and invent the emotions and inner dialogue of these children.

If that sounds outrageous, consider a fact that is well known to seasoned fiction writers: every character they develop is really another version of their multi-dimensional self. If you cannot crawl into the mind and body of a character, you cannot bring them to life on paper.

As I stated in several parts of the book, the children's thoughts, feelings, and behaviors traveled everywhere with me. They came to life in my night-dreams, creating their own plots and story lines. They were me and I was them. We resonated together.

The Excitement of Learning

After spending only a short time with Eva, I realized we were both student and teacher. When she first started to respond to the letters and words—how they were written, what they sounded like, how they appeared visually and tangibly in 3-D... *how they felt inside,* I relived the excitement of my own early learning discoveries. Each word had a meaning and I knew what that meaning was... how amazing was that!!

I tasted those 'apples' and 'oranges,' smelled the chalk and chalkboard, the wooden pencil and paper. I copied my teacher's example, shaping each letter as my fingers held the pencil just so.

I was witnessing a breakthrough with children who had been programmed by the harsh reality of rejection to believe "they couldn't do it" or "they would never get it right." It was this awakening, this excitement that I was eager to transmit to others. I started to keep a journal that would eventually become this book. My intention was to invite my readers to dip their toes into these children's first experiences of self-discovery so they could feel that buzz of excitement they had once felt themselves. I also wanted to demonstrate how much more can be accomplished when we are in an atmosphere of love and acceptance than in one of fear and rejection.

When Eva and Beverly started to feel good about themselves—when they started to develop self-esteem—they no longer needed to cover their eyes and pretend to be invisible. Now they wanted to *see others, see themselves*—and share the self with others. I felt a great personal victory when each of the children started to take pride in their accomplishments and greet the world with laughter and joy.

The children also taught me how to become a better listener, how to pay attention to the stories they told me about their inner lives. I learned *not* to try to 'understand' or untangle these stories but to embrace them as new ways of seeing and being. Dreams and inner adventures are the stuff of art, music, and poetry.

Every day I spent with these children taught me more about their amazing worlds of fantasy where everything is possible. Even though I played the role of disciplinarian in order to guide them through the labyrinths of inner and outer connection—the difference between reality and illusion—the children taught me how to shed my cloak of judgment so I could view each situation from their perspective.

I discovered that imagination and play were the way into their worlds. By my acceptance of these children's unique traits and customs and by learning their language and participating in their world and their fantasies, I was able to reach them. Once that happened, I could then show them my world of language, mathematics, socialization, and other forms of instruction. Once trust and faith were established, they were more willing to take that leap into my world of loving, caring, sharing, and learning.

Unwittingly I showed them what these experiences felt like. I invited them to try on each of them to see if it would fit into their microcosms. Often I was as surprised as they were when they burst out with: "I love you, Miss Tina." or when Ricardo, who had so often demonstrated angry, resentful, anti-social behavior, suddenly expressed genuine concern for Warren when he witnessed Warren physically injuring himself.

By demonstrating my values of self-love, love for others, self-esteem, self-confidence, and self-acceptance through laughter, fun, and play, I didn't ask or tell the children to imitate me, although I could have predicted this would be inevitable. I merely showed them a better way to respond and a better way to feel.

When they discovered that their own demonstrations of these values did not intrude on their inner worlds or cause them to fall apart, they started to take pride in their accomplishments. As soon as they became excited and curious about everything that lay behind the previously closed doors of learning that they were opening through their own efforts, their fears started to slip away.

The other interesting phenomenon that each of these children witnessed was the fact that "where there is light there can be no darkness." Imagine Beverly's joy when she discovered she could light up the whole classroom with a mere flick of the switch! Was she not lighting up her heart and her whole self at the same time? "Look what I did, all by myself!"

Martin's extraordinary talents as a storyteller and entertainer only needed to be acknowledged and recognized as an important part of who he was rather than negating them and silencing him. Imagine our great loss if we had tried to destroy the spirit of some of our greatest writers, poets, musicians and artists. We would not have many of their "Martin-works" today.

We continuously reap the benefits from individuals with special needs in literature, animal husbandry, business, music, film, mathematics, science, art and so much more. The time has come to celebrate differences rather than ignore or minimize their worth. I sincerely hope that *More Heaven* brings us closer to that understanding and acceptance so we can truly create a haven on earth for all beings to flourish and soar.

About the Author

At the age of nine, I was imprinted forever. My mother and I went into a diner for lunch in Queens, New York. Just ahead of us in the queue, another mother and her daughter waited patiently. The girl and I seemed to be the same age. The only outward difference between us was that she sat in a wheelchair and her head bobbed from side to side. When the hostess came over to the line, she looked past the woman and child, ignoring them and glanced quickly over to my mother.

"How many?" she inquired.

My mother replied that we were not first, but the hostess acted like she didn't hear her and repeated the question. When my mother asked the hostess 'why' she passed over the two people in front of us, the waitress whispered, "We don't serve people like that." The whisper was heard by everyone. The humiliated mother's face reddened and her shoulders sagged. The girl's thin body leaned to one side while her hands involuntarily jerked up and down without her control.

"Let's go, we're leaving. We won't eat in a place that discriminates against who eats here," my mother said loudly to me, making sure that everyone overheard. She turned and walked briskly out of the diner and I followed right behind her.

In that one instant, I became aware of the injustices routinely suffered by those who were different. Although I wasn't able to put it all into words at that time, I knew that I wanted in any way possible to alleviate the wrongdoing and unnecessary suffering by people who were excluded from the mainstream of society. My mother's courage and right-teaching led to my own, and that moment and many others like it permanently shaped my beliefs and values.

I also owe a lot personally and professionally to the special children I taught. What began as a curiosity when I was seventeen years old turned into a passion and led to a diversified career and a path of service that I'm truly grateful for.

At seventeen, I was a counselor in a day camp program for children with special needs. The director of the program, a courageous visionary, dared to act differently from the public sentiment, educational and social practices of the time. He created a place where exceptional children could participate in camp activities at campgrounds that also housed a program for 'normal' children. Many of the activities were self-contained and separate from the regular program. Yet, history was being made here just the same.

My heart responded to these children; the desire to help them and to make a difference in their lives was born. My career goals shifted from majoring in writing and English to special education at a New York State University. Thus was spawned an enriching professional journey into teaching, healing, public speaking, and counseling. Upon graduation, I became a special education teacher.

After completing my masters and finalizing my doctoral program, I was hired by Bancroft, as Executive Director of a comprehensive educational, clinical, vocational, autistic and residential Treatment Center for Children and Youth with special needs in New Jersey. We opened community-based programs, received state endorsement for our vocational program and began a parent training program.

With the help of colleagues, I published research regarding transition from education and the success of community-living programs. Later on, I became the Director of Research, Evaluation and Training for all the programs, including the adult program of the same facility. I was also an adjunct instructor at Temple University, teaching professionals in the education and special education departments.

Although I've moved on into private practice, my heart will always remain open to children with special needs and their families, some of which I counsel and coach today.

—Jo Anne White

Dr. Jo Anne White is an International Award-Winning, Bestselling Author and Speaker, Certified Professional Coach, Energy Master Teacher, and Business Consultant. Known globally as the "Success Doc," she gets to the heart of what matters most to organizations and people. For over two decades she's been using Success Principles to enrich the lives and businesses of her clients.

Jo Anne has helped millions of individuals and organizations shape their dreams, overcome adversity, master their own success, and triumph in business and life. Executive Producer and Host of the popular *Power Your Life* TV and Radio Shows, Dr. White has also been featured online and in national and international publications such as *CNN.com, Good Housekeeping, More, and WebMD.* She's made frequent guest appearances on Radio and Television Networks such as NBC, CBS, FOX, and Voice America. Jo Anne also serves on the Advisory Board of the Professional Woman Network and Applaud Magazine and was named a Worldwide Branding Top Female Executive in Professional Coaching by Worldwide Who's Who in 2015.

Published Books:

A Journey Within: Self-Discovery for Women

Bully Free

Emotional Wellness for Women, Vol. II & III

How to Love: Secrets to Lasting Relationships

Keys to Conscious Business Growth (2016)

Learning to Love Yourself: Self-Esteem for Women

Mastering the Art of Success

Sense Your Way to Life Satisfaction

The Teen Handbook for Self-Confidence

The Woman's Handbook for Self-Confidence

The Woman's Handbook for Self–Empowerment

Unwavering Strength, Vol. 2

Websites:

www.drjoannewhite.com

www.poweryourlifenetwork.com

www.poweredbysuccess.biz

Contact Information:

joanne@drjoannewhite.com

856-795-5854 1-877-DOC WHITE

https://www.youtube.com/user/docWhite2/videos

facebook.com/Dr.JoAnneWhite

twitter.com/JWPowerYourLife

instagram.com/JWPowerYourLife/

https://www.pinterest.com/drjoannewhite/